Preface

Welcome to *Interview Genius: Master the 100 Toughest Questions & Land Your Dream Job*. This guide is a treasure trove of insights from industry leaders and stalwarts, many of whom have shared their expertise in our magazine *Career Ahead*. Their contributions have been distilled into this book to prepare you for the wide range of challenges the interview process may present.

Understanding that each interview is unique, *Interview Genius* is designed to arm you with strategies, confidence, and the ability to tackle questions across various scenarios. Whether you're a new graduate or an experienced professional, this book aims to be an indispensable tool in your career journey.

The wisdom contained within these pages comes from seasoned professionals who have navigated both sides of the interview table. Their experiences have shaped a guide that goes beyond just answering questions; it's about presenting your authentic self, embracing continuous learning, and strategically approaching your career goals.

Interview Genius invites you to engage with each chapter, applying the insights to align with your strengths and aspirations. This edition includes perspectives tailored for fresh graduates, ensuring they can effectively showcase their potential and experiences. Whether your journey includes internships, academic projects, or early career roles, you will find guidance that resonates with your path.

Thank you for allowing us to accompany you on your path to success. Here's to mastering your interviews and landing your dream job.

Warm regards,

The Editorial Team at *Career Ahead*

Introduction

In today's competitive job market, acing the interview is more crucial than ever. This book is designed to transform the daunting interview process into an opportunity for you to shine. It is not merely a collection of questions and answers; it's a comprehensive guide to understanding the nuances behind each question, enabling you to articulate responses that showcase your strengths, align with your career aspirations, and resonate with potential employers.

Structured to provide a deep dive into the interview process, *Interview Genius* covers everything from the initial preparation stages to the final follow-up, ensuring you're equipped for every phase of your interview journey. We've meticulously compiled the toughest and most frequently asked questions across industries, providing detailed insights and strategies for crafting impactful answers. More than that, this guide offers a window into the interviewer's mind, helping you understand what employers are really looking for and how to position yourself as the ideal candidate.

For fresh graduates stepping into the complex world of job seeking, this book serves as an invaluable resource, demystifying the interview process and offering practical advice on navigating it with confidence. But its utility doesn't end there; even seasoned professionals will find fresh insights and techniques to enhance their interview skills, making *Interview Genius* a must-read for anyone looking to advance their career.

Each chapter is carefully designed to focus on different aspects of the interview, from articulating your unique value proposition and handling behavioural questions to negotiating job offers and everything in between. Real-world scenarios, expert tips, and actionable strategies are interwoven throughout the book, providing a rich learning experience that goes beyond the basics.

Why is *Interview Genius* essential reading for job seekers? Because in today's job market, it's not enough to be qualified – you must also be compelling. This book empowers you to present yourself in the best possible light, turning interviews into offers and aspirations into realities.

As you embark on this journey, remember that the path to success is a learning process, one that requires practice, reflection, and continual growth. This book is here to guide you every step of the way, unlocking the door to your dream job and beyond. Welcome to the first day of your future career.

Chapter 1: Self-Introduction and Background

Embarking on the journey towards your dream job, the first and foremost challenge you face is articulating who you are, what you've achieved, and where you see your career trajectory leading you. This initial phase of the interview process is not just about making a great first impression; it's about laying a solid foundation that positions you as the ideal candidate for the role.

This chapter is designed to equip you with the skills and confidence needed to navigate the opening moments of any interview with poise and clarity. Whether it's introducing yourself in a way that captivates your interviewer, articulating your professional strengths and acknowledging your weaknesses, or aligning your career aspirations with the company's vision, we will cover it all.

The questions explored here are universally regarded as staples in the interview process. Despite their seemingly straightforward nature, they offer a profound opportunity to differentiate yourself from other candidates. Through detailed explanations and carefully crafted sample answers, we will guide you on how to weave your experiences, skills, and aspirations into a narrative that resonates with your interviewers.

Understanding the intention behind each question and mastering the art of response will not only set you up for success in the early stages of the interview but will also build a strong rapport with your potential employer, demonstrating that you are not just another candidate – you are the candidate they have been searching for.

Let's dive into the essentials of self-presentation and background discussion, laying the first stone on your path to career advancement and fulfilment.

Q1: Tell me about yourself.

Explanation: This is your chance to make a great first impression. It's an opportunity to summarize your professional background, highlight your achievements, and share your career aspirations. Focus on what makes you unique and how your journey aligns with the job you're applying for.

Sample Answer 1: "I'm a dedicated software engineer with over six years of experience specializing in machine learning and data analysis. Throughout my career, I've successfully designed and implemented algorithms that improved data processing speeds by 40%. I'm passionate about utilizing technology to solve complex problems and am excited about the potential to bring my expertise in AI development to [Company Name]'s innovative projects."

Sample Answer 2: "As a marketing manager with a decade's experience in the fashion industry, I've led numerous campaigns that increased brand visibility and sales by over 30%. My strength lies in crafting strategic marketing plans that resonate with target audiences and drive engagement. I'm drawn to [Company Name] because of your commitment to sustainability and innovation, and I'm eager to contribute to your team by leveraging my background in eco-conscious marketing strategies."

Fresh Graduate: "I'm a recent graduate with a degree in [Your Specialization] from XYZ University. During my time in college, I completed an internship at ABC Corporation, where I [specific tasks or achievements, e.g., assisted in market research, developed a strategy to improve customer retention]. Additionally, I was part of a team project that [specific project, e.g., created a comprehensive business plan for a start-up, developed a mobile app]. These experiences have given me a solid foundation in [relevant skills, e.g., business strategy, software development, team collaboration]."

Q2: How did you hear about this position?

Explanation: This question gives insight into how actively engaged and interested you are in the role and the company. It's also a chance for interviewers to gauge the effectiveness of their recruitment channels.

Sample Answer 1: "I learned about this position through your company's career page. I regularly visit it as I'm keenly interested in opportunities that align with my skills and values, particularly in the renewable energy sector. Your company's leadership in sustainability initiatives is truly inspiring, and I'm excited about the chance to contribute to such meaningful work."

Sample Answer 2: "A colleague of mine, who is an industry contact and a current employee at [Company Name], recommended this position to me. Knowing my interest in leveraging technology for social good, she thought this role would be a perfect fit. After researching your projects and impact, I was compelled to apply."

Fresh Graduate: "I learned about this position through my university's career services center. They have a strong partnership with your company, and I attended a campus presentation where I was impressed by the innovative projects your team is working on."

Q3: What do you know about our company?

Explanation: This question tests your research and genuine interest in the company. A well-informed answer can show your enthusiasm for the role and how you might fit within the company culture and contribute to its goals.

Sample Answer 1: "I've been following [Company Name] for years and am impressed with your commitment to innovation in the tech industry. Your recent development of [Product/Service] that addresses [specific problem] is groundbreaking. It's clear that your team is at the forefront of [industry], making significant contributions that extend beyond profit, which aligns perfectly with my professional ethics and aspirations."

Sample Answer 2: "[Company Name]'s approach to customer service and its dedication to creating an unmatched user experience are well known in the industry. Your initiative [Name of Initiative] that focuses on [specific goal] particularly stands out to me. It demonstrates a level of commitment to [value or mission] that is rare, and it's something I am very eager to be a part of."

Fresh Graduate: "I know that your company is a leader in [specific industry, e.g., renewable energy solutions, financial services, technology innovation], and you've recently launched a new initiative focusing on [specific initiative, e.g., sustainable urban development, digital transformation, customer experience enhancement]. I am particularly excited about your commitment to [specific value, e.g., innovation, environmental stewardship, customer satisfaction], which aligns with my personal values and career aspirations."

Q4: Why do you want this job?

Explanation: Interviewers are looking for candidates who are passionate about the role and the company. Highlight how your skills, experiences, and career goals align with what the position and the company offer.

Sample Answer 1: "I want this job because it combines my expertise in [specific skill] with my passion for [industry or mission]. Your team's work in [specific project or field] is exactly the kind of environment where I can make a significant impact. Moreover, [Company Name]'s culture of encouraging continuous learning and innovation is where I see myself thriving and contributing to the team's success."

Sample Answer 2: "This position represents a unique opportunity to further my career in an exciting and innovative direction. The role's focus on [specific task or project] aligns perfectly with my professional experience and my personal interest in [related interest].
Additionally, working for [Company Name], a leader in [field], would offer me the challenging environment I

seek, where my contributions can directly support the company's mission to [company's mission or goal]."

Fresh Graduate: "I am drawn to this job because it offers the perfect blend of challenges and opportunities for growth in [specific field, e.g., environmental science, finance, software development], which I am passionate about. Your company's focus on [specific aspect, e.g., sustainability, innovation, customer service] resonates with my personal goals, and I am eager to contribute my skills and learn from your talented team."

Q5: Why should we hire you?

Explanation: This is your moment to shine and to articulate clearly why you are the best fit for the job. Focus on your unique selling points, including relevant skills, experiences, and demonstrated successes that directly relate to the job description.

Sample Answer 1: "You should hire me because of my comprehensive experience in [field] and my proven track record of [specific achievement]. For instance, at my last job, I [specific contribution], which resulted in [specific outcome]. I bring a combination of skills that I believe uniquely qualifies me for this role, including [skill], [skill], and [skill], all of which will enable me to contribute effectively to [Company Name]'s goals."

Sample Answer 2: "My unique blend of experience in both [area] and [area], combined with my passion for [industry or topic], makes me a strong candidate for this position. I have consistently delivered [specific results] in my previous roles and have developed [specific skill] that will be particularly beneficial for the projects [Company Name] is working on. I am eager to bring my expertise to your team and help drive [specific goal or project] to success."

Fresh Graduate: "You should hire me because I bring a strong foundation in [relevant skills, e.g., data analysis, marketing strategies, project management] and a passion for [specific field or mission, e.g., sustainable solutions, customer engagement]. During my internship, I developed [specific project or tool, e.g., a data visualization tool, a marketing campaign] that improved [specific outcome, e.g., reporting efficiency, customer engagement] by [percentage or result, e.g., 30%]. My academic projects have equipped me with the skills necessary to contribute effectively to your team, and I am eager to apply my knowledge in a real-world setting."

Q6: What are your greatest professional strengths?

Explanation: This question allows you to discuss the attributes that make you valuable to any team. Choose strengths that are most relevant to the job you're applying for and be prepared to provide examples that demonstrate how you've applied these strengths in a professional setting.

Sample Answer 1: "My greatest professional strengths include my analytical thinking, which enables me to tackle complex problems effectively, and my communication skills, which help me convey ideas clearly and collaborate efficiently with team members.

For example, in my last role, I led a project where these skills were crucial in identifying a solution that saved the company significant time and resources."

Sample Answer 2: "Leadership and resilience are among my key strengths. I've successfully managed diverse teams under tight deadlines, ensuring we stay motivated and focused on our goals. A specific instance was when my team was facing a challenging project with a tight turnaround. My leadership helped navigate the team through the project, delivering quality results on time and receiving commendation from our client."

Fresh Graduate: "My greatest strengths are [specific strengths, e.g., analytical thinking, attention to detail, leadership]. In my final year project, I led a team to [specific achievement, e.g., analyze large datasets to identify trends, develop a marketing strategy]. This project required [specific skills, e.g., meticulous attention to detail, strong analytical skills], both of which I will bring to this role."

Q7: What do you consider to be your weaknesses?

Explanation: Everyone has areas for improvement, and this question tests your self-awareness and honesty. It's also an opportunity to show that you're proactive about personal development. Choose a real weakness but also talk about the steps you're actively taking to improve.

Sample Answer 1: "I've noticed that I can be overly critical of my work, which sometimes slows down my progress. I'm addressing this by setting more realistic standards for myself and seeking timely feedback from peers to gain perspective. This approach has helped me become more efficient while maintaining high-quality work."

Sample Answer 2: "Earlier in my career, public speaking was a challenge for me. Recognizing its importance, I've taken several workshops and sought opportunities to present at team meetings. With practice, I've significantly improved my presentation skills and am now much more comfortable speaking in front of groups."

Fresh Graduate: "I sometimes struggle with [specific weakness, e.g., delegating tasks] because I like to ensure everything is done perfectly. However, I've been working on improving this by [specific actions, e.g., practicing trust in team settings, recognizing the strengths of my peers]. In my recent group project, I made a conscious effort to delegate tasks and it significantly improved our efficiency."

Q8: What is your greatest professional achievement?

Explanation: This question gives you the chance to share a highlight from your career that you are particularly proud of. Choose an achievement that is relevant to the job you're applying for and explains the impact your work had on your previous employer.

Sample Answer 1: "My greatest professional achievement was when I led a team to develop a new software feature that addressed a major customer pain point, resulting in a 40% increase in customer satisfaction scores. This project not only boosted our product's market position but also taught me valuable lessons in user-centered design and teamwork."

Sample Answer 2: "Launching a marketing campaign that increased company revenue by 25% within six months is my most significant achievement. I conceptualized the campaign strategy, led the creative direction, and monitored its execution. This experience honed my strategic planning and execution skills, and the campaign's success was a proud moment for both me and the team."

Fresh Graduate: "My greatest achievement was leading a team project to [specific achievement, e.g., develop a business plan, create a marketing campaign] that won [specific award or recognition, e.g., first place in our university's annual competition]. This project not only honed my [specific skills, e.g., technical skills, leadership, project management abilities] but also provided valuable experience in [specific area]."

Q9: Describe a challenge or conflict you've faced at work, and how you dealt with it.

Explanation: Employers ask this to assess your problem-solving skills and how you handle workplace disagreements or challenges. Focus on a situation where you took a constructive approach to resolve the issue, emphasizing the positive outcome or what you learned.

Sample Answer 1: "I once faced a situation where a project was at risk due to differing opinions on the project's direction. I organized a meeting for all stakeholders to voice their concerns and used their feedback to devise a compromise that satisfied everyone. This not only kept the project on track but also strengthened the team's collaboration."

Sample Answer 2: "In a previous role, I dealt with a conflict between two team members that was affecting morale. I facilitated a mediation session where they could communicate their issues in a controlled environment. This approach helped clear misunderstandings, restored team harmony, and taught me the value of proactive conflict resolution."

Fresh Graduate: "During my internship, our team faced a challenge when [specific challenge, e.g., a critical component of our project failed just days before the deadline]. I organized a meeting to quickly assess the situation and brainstorm solutions. We decided to reallocate resources and work overtime to fix the issue. Our teamwork and quick thinking paid off, and we delivered the project on time."

Q10: Where do you see yourself in five years?

Explanation: With this question, interviewers want to gauge your ambition, career planning, and whether your future goals align with the company's direction. Your answer should reflect a realistic progression from the role you're applying for.

Sample Answer 1: "In five years, I see myself as a senior [position], where I can contribute to strategic decisions and mentor junior team members. I am particularly interested in [specific area of expertise or project], and I believe [Company Name] provides a great platform for professional growth in this direction."

Sample Answer 2: "Five years from now, I aim to have developed a deep expertise in [field/technology] and to have taken on leadership roles on major projects. I'm excited about the prospect of growing within [Company Name], leveraging my skills to contribute to innovative solutions and company growth."

Fresh Graduate: "In five years, I see myself in a [specific role, e.g., senior analyst, project manager, team leader] in your company, contributing to strategic decisions and leading innovative projects. I am particularly interested in continuing my education and earning a professional certification in [specific field, e.g., data science, project management] to enhance my skills further. I am excited about the growth opportunities within your organization and look forward to contributing to its success."

Chapter 2: Skills and Experiences

As you navigate through the interview process, articulating your skills and experiences becomes paramount. This chapter delves into how to showcase your professional background and the unique skills that make you the ideal candidate for the role. It's about translating your past achievements into compelling narratives that resonate with your potential employers.

In this chapter, we focus on the questions that allow you to demonstrate the breadth and depth of your professional journey. This is your opportunity to discuss the tangible contributions you've made in previous roles, the skills you've honed, and how these experiences have prepared you for the challenges of the position you're applying for.

Through detailed explanations and strategic sample answers, we will guide you on highlighting your most relevant experiences, discussing your skill set with confidence, and connecting your professional background to the needs of the company and the specifics of the job description. Let's explore how to effectively communicate your professional narrative.

Q1: What specific skills do you bring to this position?

Explanation: This question aims to gauge whether your skill set aligns with the job requirements. It's crucial to focus on skills that are most relevant to the role and provide concrete examples that demonstrate your proficiency.

Sample Answer 1: "I bring a robust analytical skill set, honed through years of experience in data analysis and financial modeling. For instance, at my previous job, I developed a model that predicted sales trends with 95% accuracy, enabling our team to make informed inventory decisions. This skill will be instrumental in analyzing market trends for [Company Name] and driving strategic decisions."

Sample Answer 2: "My expertise in software development, especially in Python and JavaScript, aligns perfectly with the needs of this role. At [Previous Company], I led a project to develop a web application that improved client engagement by 40%. My technical skills, combined with my experience in leading development projects, will allow me to contribute significantly to your team."

Fresh Graduate: "I bring a solid foundation in various skills from my coursework and internships, such as [data analysis, project management, marketing strategies, etc.]. For example, during my internship at ABC Corporation, I developed a tool that improved our team's efficiency by 20%. Additionally, my final year project involved managing a team to deliver a comprehensive strategy, which helped me hone my leadership and organizational skills."

Q2: Can you describe a time when you used your expertise to solve a difficult problem?

Explanation: Interviewers are interested in how you apply your knowledge and skills to real-world situations. This question allows you to showcase your problem-solving abilities and the impact of your solutions.

Sample Answer 1: "At my last job, we faced a significant challenge with a product launch timeline due to unforeseen supply chain issues. Using my expertise in project management and my ability to negotiate with suppliers, I restructured the project timeline and sourced alternative suppliers, ensuring the launch went ahead with minimal delay."

Sample Answer 2: "Recently, I tackled a security breach that threatened sensitive client data. Leveraging my cybersecurity skills, I quickly identified and isolated the breach, then implemented additional security measures to prevent future incidents. This experience not only solved an immediate problem but also improved our overall security posture."

Fresh Graduate: "During my internship at XYZ Inc., we faced a challenge when our primary tool failed just days before a critical deadline. I used my knowledge from coursework and previous projects to develop an alternative solution, which allowed us to meet our deadline successfully. This experience taught me the importance of being resourceful and adaptable."

Q3: What professional achievement are you most proud of?

Explanation: This question allows you to highlight a significant accomplishment in your career. Choose an achievement that demonstrates your ability to deliver results, showing your potential value to the employer.

Sample Answer 1: "I'm most proud of leading a team to develop an innovative mobile application that won an industry award for its user interface design. This project was particularly challenging due to its ambitious goals and tight timeline, but it was incredibly rewarding to see our hard work recognized and appreciated by the wider industry."

Sample Answer 2: "My greatest professional achievement was implementing a new inventory management system that reduced operational costs by 20%. This project required extensive cross-departmental collaboration and a deep understanding of our logistical challenges. It was a significant milestone that underscored my commitment to continuous improvement and operational excellence."

Fresh Graduate: "I am most proud of leading a team project that won first place in our university's annual competition. This project involved extensive research, planning, and teamwork. It not only honed my analytical and strategic thinking but also showcased my ability to lead a team and deliver high-quality work under pressure."

Q4: How do you keep your skills and knowledge up to date in your field?

Explanation: Employers value candidates who are committed to lifelong learning and staying abreast of industry trends and technological advancements. This question is an opportunity to demonstrate your initiative and dedication to professional growth.

Sample Answer 1: "I'm committed to continuous learning through various channels. I regularly attend industry conferences, participate in relevant webinars, and take online courses to enhance my skill set. For instance, I recently completed a course on AI and machine learning, areas that are increasingly important in my field. This habit not only keeps my skills current but also fuels my innovation and creativity in projects."

Sample Answer 2: "Staying updated is crucial in my profession, so I dedicate time each week to reading industry journals and follow thought leaders on social media. Additionally, I'm part of a professional network where we share insights and challenges, providing me with diverse perspectives. These activities ensure I remain at the forefront of emerging trends and best practices."

Fresh Graduate: "I stay updated by regularly reading industry journals, attending webinars, and participating in online courses. For example, I recently completed a certification through an online platform, which has equipped me with the latest tools and techniques in the field. Additionally, I am an active member of professional groups on LinkedIn, where I engage in discussions and share insights with peers."

Q5: Describe a project or situation where your leadership made a difference.

Explanation: This question seeks to uncover your leadership style and your ability to influence outcomes positively. Highlight a scenario where your leadership contributed to the project's success, focusing on your actions and the impact they had.

Sample Answer 1: "In my previous role, I led a project team that was struggling with low morale and missed deadlines. By implementing regular check-ins and fostering an environment where everyone felt heard, we not only improved team morale but also increased productivity. The project was not only completed on time but also received high praise from stakeholders for its quality."

Sample Answer 2: "I once took the initiative to lead a cross-functional team to address a critical bottleneck in our production process. My leadership involved coordinating efforts across departments, facilitating communication, and driving the project towards a creative solution. The result was a 30% increase in production efficiency, showcasing the impact of effective leadership and collaboration."

Fresh Graduate: "In my final year at university, I led a team of students in a project to develop a campaign for a local non-profit. By organizing regular meetings, setting clear goals, and ensuring everyone had a voice, we created a successful campaign that increased the non-profit's visibility and donations by 25%. My leadership helped keep the team motivated and focused, resulting in a positive outcome for our client."

Q6: How do you approach teamwork and collaboration?

Explanation: Employers are looking for candidates who can work effectively within a team setting. This question allows you to discuss your interpersonal skills and how you contribute to a positive and productive team environment.

Sample Answer 1: "I approach teamwork with an open mind and a focus on clear communication. I believe in leveraging the diverse strengths of team members to achieve common goals. For example, on a recent project, I facilitated collaboration by organizing brainstorming sessions and regular updates, which helped us stay aligned and complete the project ahead of schedule."

Sample Answer 2: "Collaboration is at the heart of successful projects. I strive to build strong relationships with my team members by being approachable and supportive. In my last team, I initiated a mentorship program to share knowledge and skills, which not only enhanced our team's capabilities but also fostered a culture of continuous learning and mutual support."

Fresh Graduate: "I approach teamwork with a focus on open communication and mutual respect. During my internship at ABC Corp, I worked on a cross-functional team where clear communication and collaboration were crucial. I made sure to listen to everyone's ideas, provided constructive feedback, and contributed my own insights, which helped us successfully complete our project ahead of schedule."

Q7: Can you discuss a time when you had to adapt your work style to better meet team objectives?

Explanation: This question examines your flexibility and willingness to adjust for the greater good of the team. It's an opportunity to show that you're open-minded and can modify your approach to ensure team success.

Sample Answer 1: "On a recent project, I realized that my preference for independent work was not aligning with the team's need for more collaborative brainstorming sessions. I adapted by becoming more proactive in participating and facilitating these sessions, which not only improved the project outcome but also strengthened our team dynamics."

Sample Answer 2: "While leading a project, I noticed that my direct communication style was overwhelming some team members. To better meet our objectives, I adjusted my approach to be more inclusive and supportive, encouraging open dialogue and feedback. This change fostered a more positive team atmosphere and led to more innovative solutions."

Fresh Graduate: "While working on a group project in university, I noticed that my initial preference for independent work wasn't aligning with our team's needs for collaboration. I adapted by scheduling more group meetings and actively seeking input from my team members. This change in approach not only improved our project's outcome but also taught me the value of flexibility and team dynamics."

Q8: What do you believe are the key factors in maintaining high performance in your work?

Explanation: Through this question, interviewers want to understand what drives you and how you sustain excellence in your professional activities. Discuss the principles or practices you follow to consistently deliver high-quality work.

Sample Answer 1: "I believe that setting clear goals, maintaining a disciplined approach to time management, and continuous learning are key to high performance. Additionally, I prioritize open communication with my team and stakeholders to ensure alignment and address any issues proactively. This approach has helped me meet and exceed expectations in my projects."

Sample Answer 2: "For me, high performance is achieved through passion, resilience, and a focus on results. I ensure that I'm always challenging myself to improve and seeking feedback for development. Building strong collaborative relationships and staying focused on the customer's needs also play critical roles in maintaining high standards of excellence."

Fresh Graduate: "The key factors for maintaining high performance include setting clear goals, staying organized, and continuously seeking feedback. For instance, during my internship, I kept a detailed schedule and set daily goals to ensure I stayed on track with my tasks. Additionally, I regularly sought feedback from my supervisor to improve my work quality and efficiency."

Q9: How do you evaluate success in your work?

Explanation: This question seeks to understand your values and standards for measuring achievements, offering insights into your motivation and work ethic. It's an opportunity to discuss how you set goals, track progress, and celebrate successes.

Sample Answer 1: "I evaluate success in my work by setting clear, measurable objectives at the start of each project. Achieving these objectives is my primary measure of success. However, I also value the process of learning and growth, so I consider gaining new insights or improving skills as additional indicators of success."

Sample Answer 2: "Success for me is not just about meeting predefined goals but also about the impact of my work on the team and the broader organization. I feel successful when I contribute to a positive work environment, help my colleagues' overcome challenges, and receive positive feedback from stakeholders on my contributions."

Fresh Graduate: "I evaluate success by setting specific, measurable goals at the beginning of each project and assessing whether I have met them. For example, in my final year project, our goal was to increase engagement for a local business by 20%. We achieved a 25% increase, which I consider a success. Additionally, I value the feedback from peers and supervisors as it helps me understand the impact of my work and areas for improvement."

Q10: Tell us about a time when you had to go above and beyond to get a job done.

Explanation: This question aims to highlight your dedication, work ethic, and willingness to take the extra step when necessary. It's a chance to showcase your commitment to excellence and your ability to handle challenging situations.

Sample Answer 1: "In my previous role, we were nearing a critical product launch when a key team member fell ill. Recognizing the importance of meeting our deadline, I took on their responsibilities in addition to my own. This meant longer hours and learning new aspects of the project on the fly, but it was worth it to ensure the launch was successful and well-received by our customers."

Sample Answer 2: "During a major client presentation, we encountered unexpected technical difficulties that made our prepared material unusable. I quickly improvised by engaging the client in a discussion about their needs and how our services could be tailored to meet those needs. This approach turned a potential disaster into an opportunity, resulting in a significant contract for our company."

Fresh Graduate: "During my internship, we were nearing the deadline for a major project when a team member fell ill. I volunteered to take on additional responsibilities, working extra hours to ensure we met our deadline. This experience taught me the importance of dedication and teamwork, and our project was successfully completed on time, receiving positive feedback from our client."

Chapter 3: Work Style and Preferences

Navigating the nuances of your work style and preferences is crucial in an interview to ensure there's a mutual fit between you and the prospective employer. In this chapter, we delve into the questions that uncover how you approach your work, collaborate with others, manage challenges, and what conditions allow you to thrive professionally.

We will help you articulate your unique working style, preferences, and expectations from the workplace. It guides you on how to demonstrate your adaptability, your approach to teamwork, conflict resolution, and your strategies for staying motivated and productive.

Understanding and conveying your professional work style and preferences effectively can significantly impact the interview outcome. It assures employers that you not only have the skills and experience for the job but also the right attitude and approach to seamlessly integrate into their team and culture.

Q1: How do you prioritize your tasks?

Explanation: Employers ask this to understand your organizational skills and how you manage your workload. It's important to show that you can distinguish between urgent and important tasks and can keep track of deadlines without compromising work quality.

Sample Answer 1: "I prioritize my tasks based on urgency and impact. Each morning, I review my tasks and deadlines, then organize my day to tackle high-priority and time-sensitive tasks first. This method has helped me stay on top of my workload and consistently meet deadlines."

Sample Answer 2: "I use a combination of digital tools and traditional lists to prioritize my tasks. For long-term projects, I set milestones to ensure steady progress. For daily tasks, I assess their impact on the broader goals and prioritize accordingly, always allowing some flexibility for unforeseen issues."

Fresh Graduate: "I prioritize my tasks by assessing their urgency and impact on the overall project goals. For instance, during my internship, I used a combination of to-do lists and digital tools to organize my tasks. I would start with high-priority tasks that had tight deadlines and then move on to tasks that were important but less urgent."

Q2: Can you describe your ideal work environment?

Explanation: This question reveals your fit within the company's culture and work setting. Be honest but also flexible in your answer, highlighting how you adapt to different environments while stating your preferences.

Sample Answer 1: "My ideal work environment is one that fosters creativity, collaboration, and continuous learning. I thrive in spaces where open communication and team support are encouraged, but I also value the ability to have focused, quiet times for deep work."

Sample Answer 2: "I prefer an environment that is dynamic and fast-paced, where innovation is encouraged, and we are pushed to find solutions to challenging problems. However, I've also learned to adapt to more structured settings, finding ways to maintain agility and creativity within set parameters."

Fresh Graduate: "My ideal work environment is one that fosters collaboration and continuous learning. I thrive in settings where there is open communication and team support, but I also appreciate having some quiet time for focused work. Flexibility and opportunities for professional growth are also important to me."

Q3: How do you manage work-life balance?

Explanation: Employers want to know if you can handle job pressures without burning out. Discuss strategies you use to maintain balance, showing that you can be productive at work while also taking care of your well-being.

Sample Answer 1: "I manage work-life balance by setting clear boundaries between my professional and personal time. I prioritize my health through regular exercise and downtime activities. Effective time management and delegation at work allow me to be productive while also enjoying quality time with family and friends."

Sample Answer 2: "I believe in the importance of work-life integration, where I can be flexible with my work and personal activities based on priorities of the day. I use planning tools to ensure I meet my professional responsibilities while also dedicating time to personal development and relaxation."

Fresh Graduate: "I manage work-life balance by setting clear boundaries between my professional and personal time. I prioritize my health through regular exercise and downtime activities. Effective time management and delegation at work allow me to be productive while also enjoying quality time with family and friends."

Q4: How do you handle stress and pressure at work?

Explanation: This question assesses your resilience and coping mechanisms. Employers are looking for candidates who can remain calm and effective under pressure.

Sample Answer 1: "I handle stress by staying organized and keeping a positive outlook. I break down tasks into manageable steps and focus on what can be done immediately. Regular physical activity and mindfulness practices help me maintain mental clarity and resilience."

Sample Answer 2: "Under pressure, I focus on clear communication with my team and superiors to set realistic expectations and request support if needed. This approach, coupled with prioritization and time management, helps me navigate stressful periods successfully."

Fresh Graduate: "I handle stress by staying organized and keeping a positive outlook. I break down tasks into manageable steps and focus on what can be done immediately. Regular physical activity and mindfulness practices help me maintain mental clarity and resilience."

Q5: Describe how you approach decision-making.

Explanation: Your decision-making process is critical to employers, as it reflects your judgment, analytical skills, and ability to act with confidence.

Sample Answer 1: "My approach to decision-making involves gathering all relevant information and considering the potential outcomes. I often consult with colleagues for additional perspectives. This methodical process ensures that my decisions are well-informed and aligned with the company's goals."

Sample Answer 2: "I approach decision-making with a balance of analytical thinking and intuition. After analyzing the data and potential impacts, I trust my judgment based on past experiences to make the final call. This blend has guided me through numerous successful decisions."

Fresh Graduate: "My approach to decision-making involves gathering all relevant information and considering the potential outcomes. I often consult with colleagues for additional perspectives. This methodical process ensures that my decisions are well-informed and aligned with the project goals."

Q6: What motivates you to perform at your best?

Explanation: Understanding what drives you gives employers insight into how they can help you thrive. Highlight motivators that align with the role and company culture.

Sample Answer 1: "I'm motivated by challenging projects that push me to learn and grow. The opportunity to contribute to meaningful work that has a positive impact is incredibly rewarding. Recognition and constructive feedback also motivate me to continuously improve."

Sample Answer 2: "Working in a team-oriented environment where everyone is committed to excellence drives me to perform at my best. I'm also motivated by clear goals and the autonomy to find the best path to achieve them, as it allows me to use my skills creatively."

Fresh Graduate: "I'm motivated by challenging projects that push me to learn and grow. The opportunity to contribute to meaningful work that has a positive impact is incredibly rewarding. Recognition and constructive feedback also motivate me to continuously improve."

Q7: How do you manage conflicting priorities?

Explanation: This question tests your ability to navigate complex situations and maintain productivity under competing demands. It's an opportunity to showcase your organizational, time management, and communication skills.

Sample Answer 1: "I manage conflicting priorities by first assessing the urgency and impact of each task. Communication is key, so I discuss priorities with my manager or team to ensure alignment with business goals. This approach helps me re-prioritize tasks effectively and meet critical deadlines."

Sample Answer 2: "When faced with conflicting priorities, I create a matrix to evaluate each task based on its urgency and importance. This visual representation helps me make informed decisions about where to focus my efforts. Additionally, I'm proactive in communicating any potential delays to stakeholders, offering alternative solutions when possible."

Fresh Graduate: "I manage conflicting priorities by first assessing the urgency and impact of each task. Communication is key, so I discuss priorities with my supervisor or team to ensure alignment with business goals. This approach helps me re-prioritize tasks effectively and meet critical deadlines."

Q8: Can you give an example of how you have handled a difficult colleague or team member?

Explanation: Interpersonal skills and the ability to navigate workplace relationships are crucial. Employers are interested in how you manage conflicts and maintain a positive work environment.

Sample Answer 1: "I once worked with a colleague who was resistant to new ideas and often negative. I took the initiative to understand their perspective better and found common ground on shared goals. By focusing on collaboration and open communication, we were able to transform our relationship and improve team dynamics."

Sample Answer 2: "In my previous role, a team member consistently missed deadlines, affecting our project timeline. I approached them privately to express concern and offer support. It turned out they were overwhelmed and unsure how to ask for help. Together, we developed a more manageable workload, improving their performance and our project's success."

Fresh Graduate: "During a project in my final year, we encountered unexpected changes in client requirements that required immediate attention. I quickly adjusted my work priorities by re-evaluating the project timeline and reallocating resources to meet the new demands. This flexibility ensured we delivered the project successfully."

Q9: Describe a situation where you took on a leadership role without being formally designated as a leader.

Explanation: This question assesses your natural leadership abilities and willingness to take initiative, qualities valued in any role.

Sample Answer 1: "During a critical project phase, our team leader unexpectedly had to take leave. Recognizing the potential for disruption, I stepped in to coordinate the team's efforts, delegate tasks, and communicate with stakeholders. My informal leadership helped keep the project on track and was later recognized by our management."

Sample Answer 2: "When our team was struggling with low morale and disengagement, I initiated regular check-in meetings and team-building activities. Although I wasn't the formal leader, these efforts improved communication and team cohesion, contributing to a more positive and productive work environment."

Fresh Graduate: Answer along the same lines as the sample answers above.

Q10: How do you approach learning new skills or technologies?

Explanation: In a rapidly changing work environment, adaptability and a commitment to learning are essential. This question allows you to demonstrate your growth mindset.

Sample Answer 1: "I approach learning with curiosity and enthusiasm, setting personal goals to stay motivated. I utilize a mix of resources, including online courses, webinars, and practice projects. For example, to learn a new programming language, I set a goal to build a small app, which allowed me to apply what I learned in a practical context."

Sample Answer 2: "Whenever faced with a new skill or technology, I start by breaking down the learning process into manageable steps and seeking out resources from experts in the field. Joining online forums and communities has also been invaluable for exchanging knowledge and getting support during the learning process."

Fresh Graduate: "My approach to personal and professional development is rooted in setting specific, achievable goals and actively seeking opportunities to expand my skills and knowledge. Whether it's through formal education, mentorship, or challenging projects, I'm always looking for ways to push my boundaries and grow."

Chapter 4: Teamwork and Collaboration

In today's workplace, the ability to work well with others is not just preferred; it's essential. This chapter focuses on unraveling the dynamics of working in teams, your role within a team, how you contribute to team objectives, and navigate through challenges collaboratively. It is tailored to help you articulate your experiences and approaches to teamwork, highlighting your ability to foster a collaborative environment, resolve conflicts, and drive team success.

Through thoughtful answers to common questions on teamwork and collaboration, you'll demonstrate your readiness to be an integral part of the prospective employer's team.

Q1: How do you define successful teamwork?

Explanation: This question assesses your understanding of what makes a team function effectively. It's an opportunity to discuss the values and behaviors you believe contribute to successful collaboration.

Sample Answer 1: "To me, successful teamwork is when all members are aligned towards a common goal, leveraging their unique strengths and openly communicating. It's about creating an environment where trust, respect, and mutual support thrive, leading to innovative solutions and achieving objectives efficiently."

Sample Answer 2: "Successful teamwork is defined by the ability of the team to adapt and overcome challenges together, maintaining a positive and productive work atmosphere. Success also means that each member feels valued and motivated to contribute their best, resulting in collective achievements and personal growth."

Fresh Graduate: Answer along the same lines as the sample answers above.

Q2: Describe a time when you contributed to a team's success.

Explanation: Interviewers want concrete examples of how you've positively impacted a team. Focus on a specific instance, detailing your role, actions, and the outcome.

Sample Answer 1: "In a previous project, our team was struggling to meet a deadline. I volunteered to stay late and helped redistribute the workload based on each member's strengths, including my own. This not only boosted our efficiency but also morale, and we completed the project two days early."

Sample Answer 2: "On a marketing campaign, I noticed our approach wasn't resonating with our target demographic. I suggested a new strategy based on recent market research I had conducted. By shifting our approach, we significantly improved engagement rates and exceeded our campaign objectives."

Fresh Graduate: "During a group project at university, we were tasked with developing a marketing campaign. I took the initiative to organize our meetings, set deadlines, and ensure everyone was clear on their responsibilities. By fostering a collaborative environment and encouraging open communication, we delivered a successful campaign that received high praise from our professor."

Q3: Tell me about a time you faced a conflict while working on a team. How did you handle it?

Explanation: This question explores your conflict resolution skills and ability to maintain harmony within a team. Choose an example where you played a key role in resolving a disagreement or misunderstanding.

Sample Answer 1: "I once worked with a team member who had a very different opinion on the direction of a project. Instead of letting the disagreement escalate, I proposed a meeting to discuss our viewpoints. Through open dialogue, we found a compromise that combined our ideas, enhancing the project's outcome."

Sample Answer 2: "During a team project, there was a conflict over resource allocation. I facilitated a discussion to understand each side's concerns and priorities. We agreed on a solution that involved re-evaluating our project scope and resources, which resolved the conflict and strengthened our collaboration."

Fresh Graduate: "In a team project, there was a disagreement over the direction of our research. I proposed a meeting to discuss everyone's viewpoints and find common ground. By actively listening and encouraging open dialogue, we managed to combine our ideas and enhance the overall quality of the project."

Q4: How do you encourage others in your team?

Explanation: Encouragement and motivation are crucial for team morale and productivity. Share your strategies for supporting and uplifting team members.

Sample Answer 1: "I encourage others by acknowledging their contributions and highlighting the impact of their work on our team's goals. Positive reinforcement and expressing genuine appreciation can significantly boost morale and motivation."

Sample Answer 2: "I find that setting aside time for regular one-on-one check-ins is an effective way to provide encouragement. It allows me to understand team members' challenges and offer targeted support or recognition, fostering a supportive and collaborative team environment."

Fresh Graduate: "I encourage others by recognizing their contributions and providing positive feedback. During my internship, I regularly acknowledged my teammates' efforts in meetings, which boosted morale and motivation. I also made sure to offer help and support whenever someone faced challenges."

Q5: Describe how you handle sharing credit with your team.

Explanation: This question gauges your humility and ability to recognize the contributions of others. It's important to show that you value teamwork over individual achievement.

Sample Answer 1: "I believe in openly acknowledging and celebrating the efforts of all team members. Whether it's in team meetings, in reports to management, or informal discussions, I make sure to highlight specific contributions and the collective work that led to our success."

Sample Answer 2: "Sharing credit is fundamental to a cohesive team dynamic. I always mention the roles and contributions of my team members when discussing project successes, both within the team and in communications with other departments or stakeholders. This practice reinforces a culture of appreciation and mutual respect."

Fresh Graduate: Answer along the same lines as the sample answers above.

Q6: How do you deal with a team member who isn't pulling their weight?

Explanation: This question evaluates your ability to handle difficult situations in a team setting while maintaining a constructive approach. It's crucial to balance assertiveness with empathy.

Sample Answer 1: "I address the situation by first trying to understand the underlying reasons for their performance issues in a one-on-one conversation. I offer support and resources to help them improve. If the situation doesn't change, I escalate the matter to a supervisor, ensuring the team's productivity isn't compromised."

Sample Answer 2: "I believe in open communication, so I'd gently approach the team member to discuss the issue and express concern. I'd inquire if there are external factors affecting their work and suggest potential solutions or adjustments. It's about finding a balance between upholding team standards and showing empathy."

Fresh Graduate: Answer along the same lines as the sample answers above.

Q7: What strategies do you use to build rapport with a new team?

Explanation: Employers are interested in how quickly and effectively you can integrate into existing teams. Your answer should reflect your interpersonal skills and adaptability.

Sample Answer 1: "I build rapport with new teams by taking the initiative to learn about each member's roles, strengths, and interests. I share about myself too and look for common ground. Participating actively in team meetings and offering help where needed also fosters mutual respect and camaraderie."

Sample Answer 2: "Upon joining a new team, I prioritize one-on-one meetings with each member to understand their expectations of me and how we can best work together. I also ensure I'm approachable and open to feedback, which helps in building trust and rapport quickly."

Fresh Graduate: "During a group project, I noticed my preference for independent work wasn't aligning with the team's need for more collaborative brainstorming sessions. I adapted by becoming more proactive in participating and facilitating these sessions, which improved the project's outcome and strengthened our team dynamics."

Q8: Give an example of a team project that failed. What did you learn from the experience?

Explanation: This question explores your ability to reflect on and learn from past experiences, including those that didn't have the desired outcomes. It highlights your resilience and capacity for growth.

Sample Answer 1: "In a previous role, our team worked on a project that ultimately didn't meet the client's expectations due to miscommunication about their needs. This experience taught me the importance of regular check-ins with all stakeholders and reinforced the value of clear and concise communication."

Sample Answer 2: "Our team once missed a critical deadline, leading to project failure. The setback was a learning opportunity for us to improve our project management practices. We started implementing more rigorous time tracking and progress review meetings, significantly enhancing our future project execution."

Fresh Graduate: "The key factors for maintaining high performance include setting clear goals, staying organized, and continuously seeking feedback. During my internship, I kept a detailed schedule and set daily goals to ensure I stayed on track with my tasks. Additionally, I regularly sought feedback from my supervisor to improve my work quality and efficiency."

Q9: How do you contribute to a positive team environment?

Explanation: This question assesses your ability to contribute to team morale and culture. Highlight how your actions and attitude support a collaborative and supportive work environment.

Sample Answer 1: "I contribute to a positive team environment by always maintaining a positive attitude and encouraging open communication. I acknowledge the achievements of others and provide support during challenging times, which I believe fosters a strong sense of team unity and collaboration."

Sample Answer 2: "By being an active listener and showing empathy towards my team members, I help create a supportive atmosphere. I also initiate team-building activities that not only boost morale but also help us understand each other's working styles better, contributing to a more cohesive team."

Fresh Graduate: "I evaluate success by setting specific, measurable goals at the beginning of each project and assessing whether I have met them. Additionally, I value feedback from peers and supervisors as it helps me understand the impact of my work and areas for improvement."

Q10: What do you think are the key factors in maintaining effective team dynamics?

Explanation: This question delves into your understanding of what makes a team function well together. It's an opportunity to discuss the principles you believe are essential for healthy team dynamics.

Sample Answer 1: "Effective team dynamics are built on trust, respect, and open communication. Setting clear goals and roles for each team member, while fostering an environment where feedback is freely exchanged, are key factors. Celebrating successes together also strengthens team bonds."

Sample Answer 2: "The key factors include mutual respect among team members, transparent communication, and a clear understanding of common goals. Additionally, recognizing and valuing the diverse skills and perspectives each member brings to the team enhances collaboration and innovation."

Fresh Graduate: Answer along the same lines as the sample answers above.

Chapter 5: Leadership and Management

Leadership and management capabilities are in high demand across all levels of professional roles, not just those explicitly titled as managerial. This chapter is designed to help you articulate your leadership style, experiences, and philosophy, whether you've led a team formally or have taken the lead on projects or initiatives. This chapter delves into how you inspire, guide, and drive others towards achieving common goals while navigating the complexities of team dynamics and organizational objectives.

Through a series of targeted questions, we aim to reveal your potential as a leader or manager, showcasing your ability to motivate, delegate, resolve conflicts, and contribute to a positive and productive work culture. Whether you're aspiring to move into a leadership role or seeking to highlight your existing managerial prowess, the insights and sample answers provided here will equip you with the tools to demonstrate your leadership qualities confidently.

Q1: How would you describe your leadership style?

Explanation: This question aims to understand how you guide and inspire others. It's your chance to share your philosophy on leadership and how it plays out in practice.

Sample Answer 1: "I describe my leadership style as collaborative and empowering. I believe in setting clear goals and expectations, then giving my team the autonomy to determine how best to achieve them. This fosters innovation and accountability, allowing team members to grow and excel."

Sample Answer 2: "My leadership style is adaptive, recognizing that different situations and team members may require different approaches. I strive to lead by example, maintaining open lines of communication and providing support where needed, while encouraging my team to push boundaries and take ownership of their work."

Fresh Graduate: "As a fresh graduate, my leadership style is collaborative and supportive. I focus on setting clear goals and expectations while encouraging open communication and teamwork. I believe in leading by example, showing dedication and a positive attitude to inspire others."

Q2: Can you share an experience where you successfully led a team through a challenging situation?

Explanation: Employers are interested in leaders who can navigate through adversity. Highlight an instance where your leadership made a significant positive impact.

Sample Answer 1: "During a critical product launch, we encountered significant technical issues that threatened our timeline. As the project leader, I organized emergency meetings, delegated tasks based on team members' strengths, and liaised with stakeholders to manage expectations. Through teamwork and resilience, we resolved the issues and launched successfully."

Sample Answer 2: "Faced with a sudden budget cut, I had to lead my team through a restructuring of our project plan. By prioritizing essential tasks and exploring creative alternatives for non-essential ones, we not only met our objectives but also discovered more efficient ways of working that we continued to use."

Fresh Graduate: "During my final year project, our team faced a tight deadline and unexpected [technical/logistical] challenges. I organized additional meetings to brainstorm solutions and redistributed tasks based on each member's strengths. This collaborative approach helped us complete the project on time and with high quality."

Q3: How do you motivate your team?

Explanation: This question explores your ability to inspire and engage your team members, ensuring they're committed to their work and the team's goals.

Sample Answer 1: "I motivate my team by ensuring that each member understands how their work contributes to the broader company objectives. Recognizing achievements, providing opportunities for professional development, and fostering a supportive team environment are key strategies I use."

Sample Answer 2: "Motivation comes from within, so I spend time understanding my team members' personal and professional goals and aligning them with project tasks. Regular feedback and celebrating milestones, both big and small, help maintain high morale and motivation."

Fresh Graduate: "I motivate my team by recognizing individual contributions and ensuring everyone understands how their work contributes to our shared goals. I also create a positive and inclusive environment where team members feel valued and supported, encouraging them to do their best."

Q4: How do you delegate responsibilities to your team?

Explanation: Effective delegation is a critical leadership skill. This question assesses your ability to distribute tasks efficiently while considering your team members' skills, career aspirations, and workload.

Sample Answer 1: "I delegate responsibilities based on individual strengths and development goals, ensuring tasks are both challenging and achievable. I discuss the expectations and provide the necessary resources and support, then trust my team to deliver, offering guidance as needed."

Sample Answer 2: "Delegating starts with knowing my team's capabilities and interests. I match tasks to skills, providing clear objectives and deadlines. I also consider this an opportunity for team members to stretch their abilities, offering support and feedback throughout the process."

Fresh Graduate: "I delegate responsibilities by assessing each team member's strengths and interests, then assigning tasks that align with their skills and development goals. I provide clear instructions and resources, and remain available for support and guidance to ensure successful completion."

Q5: Describe your approach to handling underperformance in your team.

Explanation: Addressing underperformance is a delicate aspect of management. This question seeks insights into your ability to confront and resolve such issues constructively.

Sample Answer 1: "When addressing underperformance, my approach is to first seek to understand the root cause, whether it's a skills gap, personal issues, or unclear expectations. I then work with the team member to develop a performance improvement plan, providing support and regular check-ins to track progress."

Sample Answer 2: "I handle underperformance by having an open and honest conversation with the team member, focusing on specific areas for improvement and setting achievable goals. I offer additional training or mentoring and emphasize that my goal is to help them succeed."

Fresh Graduate: Answer along the same lines as the sample answers above.

Q6: How do you ensure your team's goals align with the overall company objectives?

Explanation: This question gauges your ability to maintain strategic alignment within your team, ensuring that everyone's efforts contribute to the broader company vision.

Sample Answer 1: "I ensure alignment by regularly reviewing company objectives and translating them into specific, measurable team goals. During team meetings, we discuss how our work fits into the larger company strategy, encouraging everyone to see the value of their contributions to the company's success."

Sample Answer 2: "I stay informed on company objectives and initiatives through communication with senior leadership and other departments. This allows me to align our team's goals and projects accordingly. I also foster a culture of transparency, where team members understand how their work directly impacts the company's growth and success."

Fresh Graduate: Answer along the same lines as the sample answers above.

Q7: Can you give an example of how you've fostered teamwork and collaboration within your team?

Explanation: Effective leadership involves creating a collaborative team environment. Share a specific instance where your actions encouraged teamwork.

Sample Answer 1: "Recognizing that our team was operating in silos, I initiated a series of cross-functional workshops where team members could share their expertise and collaborate on solutions to shared challenges. These sessions improved our team's cohesion and productivity, leading to more innovative and comprehensive project outcomes."

Sample Answer 2: "To foster collaboration, I implemented regular 'team huddle' meetings where members could discuss ongoing projects, share ideas, and offer support. This improved our project outcomes and strengthened interpersonal relationships within the team, creating a more unified and supportive work environment."

Fresh Graduate: Answer along the same lines as the sample answers above.

Q8: Describe a situation where you had to provide feedback to a team member. How did you approach it?

Explanation: This question examines your communication skills and sensitivity in providing constructive feedback to foster growth and improvement.

Sample Answer 1: "I had to provide feedback to a team member whose work had been slipping. I approached the conversation with empathy, focusing on specific areas for improvement and providing examples. I made sure to also highlight their strengths and offered my support to help them improve, turning it into a positive learning experience."

Sample Answer 2: "When providing feedback on a project that didn't meet expectations, I scheduled a one-on-one meeting to discuss it privately. I used the 'feedback sandwich' method, starting and ending with positive points and placing the constructive feedback in between. We then worked together to create an action plan for improvement."

Fresh Graduate: Answer along the same lines as the sample answers above.

Q9: How do you support the professional development of your team members?

Explanation: Leaders play a critical role in the growth and development of their team members. Explain how you encourage and facilitate their professional advancement.

Sample Answer 1: "I support my team's professional development by identifying individual learning opportunities and encouraging participation in training and workshops. I also advocate for my team's exposure to challenging projects that stretch their abilities, accompanied by regular feedback and guidance."

Sample Answer 2: "I conduct regular career development discussions with each team member to understand their aspirations and identify ways to support their growth. Whether it's through mentoring, shadowing opportunities, or external courses, I ensure they have the resources and support needed to achieve their goals."

Fresh Graduate: Answer along the same lines as the sample answers above.

Q10: How do you lead by example?

Explanation: This question seeks to understand your integrity as a leader and how you model the behaviors and values you expect from your team.

Sample Answer 1: "I lead by example by upholding the highest standards of professionalism, from punctuality and ethical decision-making to showing respect and support for my colleagues. I make sure to stay engaged and proactive in my work, demonstrating the work ethic and commitment I hope to inspire in my team."

Sample Answer 2: "I embody the values of our company and the standards I set for my team in my daily actions. This means taking responsibility for my mistakes, continually seeking feedback for improvement, and prioritizing the well-being of my team. By acting as a role model, I establish a culture of accountability and continuous growth."

Fresh Graduate: Answer along the same lines as the sample answers above.

Chapter 6: Adaptability and Problem Solving

In a rapidly changing professional landscape, adaptability and effective problem-solving skills are more crucial than ever. This chapter zeroes in on your ability to navigate uncertainty, embrace change, and tackle challenges head-on. It is designed to help you convey your flexibility, resilience, and innovation in overcoming obstacles and finding solutions.

Employers value candidates who can demonstrate a proactive approach to change and an ability to think critically under pressure. Here, you'll learn how to articulate your experiences with adaptability and problem-solving in a way that resonates with hiring managers, showcasing your readiness to thrive in dynamic environments and contribute to your future team's success.

Q1: Describe a time when you had to adapt to a significant change at work. How did you handle it?

Explanation: This question assesses your resilience and flexibility in the face of change. Highlight your ability to remain productive and positive.

Sample Answer 1: "When my company underwent a major restructuring, my role was significantly altered. I took the initiative to learn new skills relevant to my new responsibilities, sought advice from peers, and adjusted my work style to fit the new structure. My adaptability not only helped me transition smoothly but also allowed me to excel in my new role."

Sample Answer 2: "Our team had to switch to a completely remote setup due to external circumstances.

Recognizing the challenge of maintaining team cohesion, I spearheaded the implementation of regular virtual check-ins and team-building activities. My efforts helped sustain team morale and productivity during the transition."

Fresh Graduate: "During my internship, our team had to transition to remote work due to unforeseen circumstances. I adapted by setting up a dedicated workspace at home, staying in regular contact with my team through virtual meetings, and using project management tools to keep track of tasks and deadlines. This helped me stay productive and maintain team cohesion."

Q2: How do you approach solving a problem you've never encountered before?

Explanation: This question delves into your critical thinking and resourcefulness. Discuss your process for tackling unfamiliar challenges.

Sample Answer 1: "I approach new problems with an open mind and a structured process. First, I gather as much information as possible to understand the issue. Then, I brainstorm potential solutions, considering their feasibility and impact. I'm not afraid to consult with colleagues or look into past precedents for insights, ensuring a well-informed decision."

Sample Answer 2: "Facing an unfamiliar problem, I start by breaking it down into smaller, manageable components. I research each aspect, leveraging online resources and my network for advice. This methodical approach, combined with creative thinking, has enabled me to successfully resolve issues even when they were outside my immediate area of expertise."

Fresh Graduate: Answer along the same lines as the sample answers above.

Q3: Can you give an example of a creative solution you devised for a challenging problem?

Explanation: Creativity in problem-solving indicates your ability to think outside the box. Share a scenario where your innovative thinking led to a successful outcome.

Sample Answer 1: "In an effort to reduce operational costs, I proposed automating a manual, time-consuming process that was prone to errors. By developing a simple software tool, we not only cut down on errors but also saved hundreds of hours annually, significantly reducing expenses."

Sample Answer 2: "Faced with a client who was hesitant to adopt our solution due to unfamiliarity, I created an interactive, gamified demo that made the learning process engaging and intuitive. This creative approach not only won over the client but also set a new standard for how we presented our products."

Fresh Graduate: "During a group project, we faced a challenge with limited resources. I proposed using free online tools and open-source software to complete our work. This creative approach not only helped us stay within budget but also improved the quality of our project, showcasing our resourcefulness."

Q4: Describe a time when you had to quickly adjust your work priorities.

Explanation: Employers are looking for candidates who can effectively manage their workload, especially when priorities shift unexpectedly. Describe how you stay organized and responsive.

Sample Answer 1: "When a critical issue arose with a high-priority client project, I had to immediately shift my focus from another assignment. I reassessed my workload, communicated the change in priorities to relevant stakeholders, and reallocated my time to ensure the client issue was resolved swiftly, demonstrating my ability to prioritize effectively under pressure."

Sample Answer 2: "During a product launch, an unexpected bug was discovered, necessitating an immediate adjustment in my work priorities. I coordinated with the development team to address the bug while reorganizing launch tasks to keep everything on track. My quick thinking and flexibility ensured the launch was only minimally delayed."

Fresh Graduate: "While working on multiple assignments, a high-priority task suddenly came up. I immediately reassessed my workload, communicated the change in priorities to my team, and reorganized my schedule to focus on the urgent task. This quick adjustment ensured that all critical deadlines were met without compromising the quality of my work."

Q5: How do you handle failure or setbacks?

Explanation: This question explores your resilience and ability to learn from experiences. Discuss how you view failure as an opportunity for growth.

Sample Answer 1: "I view failure as a crucial learning opportunity. After a project I led did not achieve its objectives, I conducted a thorough review to identify what went wrong. This reflective process led to significant improvements in our project management approach, enhancing future project success."

Sample Answer 2: "Setbacks, while disappointing, are not deterrents for me. I take the time to analyze what led to the failure, extracting key lessons and applying them to future endeavors. This approach has helped me refine my strategies and avoid repeating the same mistakes."

Fresh Graduate: Answer along the same lines as the sample answers above.

Q6: How do you prioritize tasks when facing multiple deadlines?

Explanation: This question assesses your time management and organizational skills under pressure. It's crucial to demonstrate your ability to evaluate tasks based on urgency and importance.

Sample Answer 1: "I use a combination of the Eisenhower Matrix and agile methodologies to prioritize tasks, categorizing them based on their urgency and importance. This allows me to focus on what needs immediate attention while planning for less critical tasks.

Communication with stakeholders about timelines ensures that expectations are managed effectively."

Sample Answer 2: "When juggling multiple deadlines, I first outline all tasks and their due dates. I then assess each task's impact on the overall project or organizational goals, prioritizing accordingly. Regular check-ins with my team and stakeholders help me adjust priorities as needed, ensuring that all deadlines are met without compromising work quality."

Fresh Graduate: "I use a combination of to-do lists and digital tools to prioritize tasks, categorizing them based on their urgency and importance. This allows me to focus on what needs immediate attention while planning for less critical tasks. Communication with stakeholders about timelines ensures that expectations are managed effectively."

Q7: Tell us about a time you had to learn something new to complete a task or project.

Explanation: Employers value candidates who are proactive learners and can adapt to new knowledge or skills requirements. Highlight your commitment to self-improvement and growth.

Sample Answer 1: "For a project that required advanced knowledge of a new software, I took the initiative to enroll in an online course and spent extra hours practicing. My effort not only allowed me to contribute effectively to the project but also added valuable skills to my repertoire, which I later shared with my team."

Sample Answer 2: "When assigned to lead a project outside my expertise, I immediately began researching and seeking mentorship from knowledgeable colleagues. This accelerated learning process was challenging but ultimately rewarding, as it significantly broadened my skill set and confidence in tackling diverse projects."

Fresh Graduate: Answer along the same lines as the sample answers above.

Q8: How do you stay motivated and productive during repetitive or mundane tasks?

Explanation: This question explores your self-motivation strategies and how you maintain high performance, even in less engaging tasks.

Sample Answer 1: "I stay motivated by setting personal milestones and rewarding myself upon achieving them. I also try to find aspects of the task that I can learn from or that might challenge me in some way, turning the mundane into an opportunity for improvement."

Sample Answer 2: "To maintain productivity, I break down repetitive tasks into smaller, manageable segments and focus on completing them one at a time. Mixing in more engaging tasks throughout the day also helps keep my energy levels up. Understanding the importance of these tasks in the bigger picture helps sustain my motivation."

Fresh Graduate: Answer along the same lines as the sample answers above.

Q9: Describe a situation where you had to make a tough decision with limited information.

Explanation: Decision-making with incomplete data tests your judgment, risk assessment, and ability to act decisively. Share how you navigate these situations with confidence.

Sample Answer 1: "Faced with a tight deadline, I had to decide on a vendor with incomplete comparative data. I based my decision on available information, prioritizing reliability and past performance. Post-decision, I set up additional checkpoints to mitigate potential risks, ensuring the project remained on track."

Sample Answer 2: "When a critical team member unexpectedly left, I had to quickly redistribute their responsibilities without full insight into everyone's current workload. I made decisions based on my understanding of the team's capabilities, followed by open discussions to reallocate tasks efficiently, maintaining project momentum."

Fresh Graduate: Answer along the same lines as the sample answers above.

Q10: How do you assess and manage risks in your work?

Explanation: Understanding your approach to risk management offers insights into your strategic thinking and planning skills. It's essential to show that you can identify potential pitfalls and implement measures to mitigate them.

Sample Answer 1: "I assess risks by evaluating the likelihood of adverse outcomes and their potential impact on project goals. This involves consulting with stakeholders and conducting a thorough review of similar past projects. Based on this analysis, I develop contingency plans and monitor key risk indicators closely to mitigate issues before they escalate."

Sample Answer 2: "My approach to risk management involves a proactive analysis of all aspects of a project, identifying areas of uncertainty and their possible effects. I prioritize these risks and develop strategies to address them, such as diversifying approaches or setting aside resources for potential problem areas. Regular team discussions ensure that risk management is a shared responsibility."

Fresh Graduate: Answer along the same lines as the sample answers above.

Chapter 7: Continuous Learning and Development

In an ever-evolving professional landscape, the pursuit of knowledge and the eagerness to grow are traits that distinguish outstanding individuals. This chapter is crafted to help you communicate your commitment to self-improvement and your proactive approach to acquiring new skills and knowledge. Here, we explore how you stay abreast of industry trends, tackle learning new technologies, and apply new knowledge to enhance your work.

Employers seek candidates who not only have a solid foundation of skills but are also enthusiastic about expanding their expertise and adapting to new challenges. Through this chapter, you will learn how to articulate your dedication to continuous learning, showcasing how your growth mindset contributes to your professional success and the success of those around you.

Q1: How do you stay updated with the latest trends in your industry?

Explanation: This question assesses your initiative in maintaining relevance in your field. It's an opportunity to share your strategies for keeping abreast of new developments and technologies.

Sample Answer 1: "I stay updated by subscribing to leading industry newsletters and attending webinars and conferences. This not only keeps me informed about the latest trends but also allows me to network with peers. Additionally, I participate in online forums and discussion groups related to my field, where I can exchange ideas and insights with other professionals."

Sample Answer 2: "I make it a point to dedicate time each week to reading articles and research papers from key industry journals. I also take online courses on platforms like Coursera and LinkedIn Learning to deepen my knowledge in specific areas. Engaging with thought leaders on social media further enriches my understanding of emerging trends."

Fresh Graduate: Answer along the same lines as the sample answers above.

Q2: What professional skill are you currently working to improve?

Explanation: Highlighting your current learning endeavors shows your commitment to self-improvement and adaptability. Choose a skill that is relevant to your career goals and the position you're applying for.

Sample Answer 1: "I'm currently focused on improving my data visualization skills. With the increasing importance of data-driven decision-making, I believe that being able to present data in a clear and impactful way is crucial. I've been using tools like Tableau and taking specialized courses to enhance my proficiency in this area."

Sample Answer 2: "I am working on enhancing my project management skills, particularly in agile methodologies. Understanding that agility and flexibility are key to modern project management, I've enrolled in a certification course on Scrum and have been applying agile practices to my current projects to improve efficiency and team collaboration."

Fresh Graduate: "I'm currently focused on improving my [data visualization/communication/project management] skills. With the increasing importance of [data-driven decision-making/team collaboration/effective project execution], I believe that being able to [present data clearly/communicate effectively/manage projects efficiently] is crucial. I've been using tools like [Tableau/Microsoft Teams/Trello] and taking specialized courses to enhance my proficiency in this area."

Q3: Can you share how you've applied a new skill or knowledge at work recently?

Explanation: This question allows you to demonstrate your ability to translate learning into action. It's a chance to show how you've directly contributed to your workplace with newly acquired skills or knowledge.

Sample Answer 1: "After completing a course on machine learning, I identified an opportunity at work to apply this knowledge by developing a predictive model to optimize our inventory management. The model has significantly improved accuracy in demand forecasting, leading to better stock levels and reduced waste."

Sample Answer 2: "Recently, I learned a new programming language, Go, which I applied to streamline a critical process in our back-end system. This not only improved the process's efficiency by 30%

73

but also increased the system's reliability, showcasing my initiative and ability to enhance our operations with new technologies."

Fresh Graduate: "After completing a course on [machine learning/advanced Excel/project management], I identified an opportunity at work to apply this knowledge by [developing a predictive model/creating complex financial models/streamlining project workflows]. This has significantly improved [accuracy in demand forecasting/efficiency in reporting/team collaboration], showcasing my initiative and ability to enhance our operations with new technologies."

Q4: Describe a time when you had to learn something completely outside of your comfort zone.

Explanation: Employers value individuals who can tackle challenges head-on, even when it means stepping out of their comfort zone. Share an experience that highlights your willingness to embrace new challenges and learn.

Sample Answer 1: "I was tasked with leading a project that required knowledge of regulatory compliance, a topic I was not familiar with. I immersed myself in research and sought mentorship from experts within our organization. This effort not only broadened my expertise but also ensured the project's success and compliance with all regulations."

Sample Answer 2: "When our team needed to adopt a new software tool that was unfamiliar to me, I took the initiative to learn it thoroughly through online tutorials and practice. My proactive approach allowed me to become proficient quickly, enabling me to train my teammates and facilitate a smooth transition to the new tool."

Fresh Graduate: "I was tasked with leading a project that required knowledge of [regulatory compliance/coding in a new language/a new marketing strategy], a topic I was not familiar with. I researched online resources and sought mentorship from experts within our organization. This exercise broadened my expertise and helped the project succeed."

Q5: How do you balance the demands of work with the need to keep learning and developing?

Explanation: This question examines your time management and prioritization skills in the context of lifelong learning. Discuss how you integrate continuous learning into your busy schedule.

Sample Answer 1: "I balance work and continuous learning by setting clear priorities and being disciplined about my time. I allocate specific hours each week for professional development, whether it's reading industry articles, attending training sessions, or working on personal projects that enhance my skills."

Sample Answer 2: "I leverage the natural overlaps between my work projects and personal learning interests. This allows me to apply new knowledge directly to my work, making learning part of my daily routine. I also take advantage of company-offered training and encourage knowledge-sharing sessions with my team."

Fresh Graduate: Answer along the same lines as the sample answers above.

Q6: What role does feedback play in your professional development?

Explanation: Feedback is crucial for growth and improvement. This question explores how you perceive and utilize feedback to advance your skills and career.

Sample Answer 1: "Feedback is a cornerstone of my professional development. I actively seek it from peers, supervisors, and mentors, viewing it as a valuable resource for learning and growth. Constructive criticism helps me identify areas for improvement, while positive feedback reinforces my strengths and motivates me further."

Sample Answer 2: "I consider feedback as essential to refining my skills and performance. After receiving feedback, I reflect on it, determine actionable steps for improvement, and sometimes set up follow-up discussions to gauge my progress. This iterative process has been instrumental in achieving my career milestones."

Fresh Graduate: Answer along the same lines as the sample answers above.

Q7: How do you mentor or help others grow professionally within your team?

Explanation: This question assesses your willingness to contribute to the development of others, a key trait of a collaborative and forward-thinking professional.

Sample Answer 1: "I mentor others by sharing knowledge, providing constructive feedback, and offering support on their projects. I also encourage my mentees to tackle new challenges and pursue learning opportunities, and I make myself available for discussions and advice whenever they need it."

Sample Answer 2: "Within my team, I've initiated a peer learning program where each member shares expertise in their area of strength. By organizing these knowledge-sharing sessions, I help foster a culture of continuous learning and development, benefiting the entire team."

Fresh Graduate: Answer along the same lines as the sample answers above.

Q8: How have you applied a lesson learned from a failure or mistake in your professional life?

Explanation: Acknowledging and learning from failures is as important as celebrating successes. Share an instance where a setback led to valuable insights and subsequent improvements.

Sample Answer 1: "After a project I led didn't meet our objectives, I conducted a thorough review to identify what went wrong. The key lesson was the importance of early stakeholder engagement, which I've since applied to ensure all projects I manage are aligned with stakeholder expectations from the outset."

Sample Answer 2: "I once made an error in a client report that, fortunately, was caught before it caused any issues. This mistake highlighted the need for more rigorous data verification processes, which I helped implement. This not only improved the accuracy of our reports but also taught me the value of double-checking and verification."

Fresh Graduate: Answer along the same lines as the sample answers above.

Q9: Describe your approach to taking on new responsibilities or roles that require skills you do not yet possess.

Explanation: This question explores your approach to growth and how you handle transitions that push you beyond your current capabilities.

Sample Answer 1: "When facing new responsibilities that require unfamiliar skills, I adopt a proactive learning approach. I identify key resources, such as courses or experts within the organization, to quickly get up to speed. I'm also open about my learning process with my team, fostering an environment where seeking help and continuous improvement is valued."

Sample Answer 2: "I approach such challenges with enthusiasm and an open mind. I start by breaking down the new skills into manageable learning objectives and prioritizing them based on the demands of the role. Engaging with mentors and applying new knowledge in practical scenarios accelerates my learning and builds my confidence in the new responsibilities."

Fresh Graduate: Answer along the same lines as the sample answers above.

Q10: How do you measure the impact of your personal development efforts on your professional performance?

Explanation: This question seeks to understand how you evaluate the effectiveness of your continuous learning endeavors in contributing to your work.

Sample Answer 1: "I measure the impact of my development efforts by setting specific, measurable goals related to my learning and how it applies to my job. For example, after learning a new software, I track improvements in my project completion times or the reduction of errors. Feedback from peers and supervisors also provides valuable insights into my progress."

Sample Answer 2: "The impact of my personal development is measured through the quality of my work, my ability to tackle more complex projects, and the feedback I receive from colleagues and clients. I also reflect on my professional journey, noting milestones achieved through new skills or knowledge, to gauge my growth and identify future learning paths."

Fresh Graduate: Answer along the same lines as the sample answers above.

Chapter 8: Innovation and Creativity

In the ever-evolving landscape of modern industries, innovation and creativity stand out as critical skills that can drive businesses forward and solve complex challenges. This chapter focusses on showcasing your ability to think outside the box, bring fresh ideas to the table, and foster an environment that encourages experimentation and growth. Here you will learn to articulate your experiences with innovation and creative problem-solving in a way that highlights your contribution to fostering progress and efficiency within your teams and projects.

Employers value candidates who not only possess technical skills and knowledge but also demonstrate the capacity to approach problems with a creative mindset and propose innovative solutions. Through this chapter, you'll learn how to effectively communicate your creativity and innovative approach, emphasizing how your unique perspective and inventive ideas can contribute to the success of the organization.

Q1: Can you describe a situation where you had to think creatively to solve a problem?

Explanation: This question assesses your ability to use creativity in overcoming obstacles and achieving goals. It's an opportunity to demonstrate your innovative thinking and its impact on results.

Sample Answer 1: "Faced with a product development deadline and budget constraints, I held a brainstorming session with my team to find cost-effective alternatives to our initial plan. This creative exercise resulted in discovering a new material that not only reduced costs but also improved the product's durability, highlighting the value of thinking creatively under pressure."

Sample Answer 2: "When our traditional marketing strategies were not yielding expected results, I proposed a guerrilla marketing campaign that was unconventional but highly engaging. By thinking creatively and taking a risk, we significantly increased our brand visibility and customer engagement within a tight budget."

Fresh Graduate: Answer along the same lines as the sample answers above.

Q2: How do you foster innovation within your team or organization?

Explanation: Employers look for leaders who can inspire and cultivate an innovative culture. Share your strategies for encouraging creativity and experimentation among your team members.

Sample Answer 1: "I foster innovation by creating an open environment where every team member feels safe to share their ideas, no matter how unconventional. I regularly organize 'innovation labs' where we collaboratively explore new ideas without fear of failure, encouraging a mindset that views challenges as opportunities for innovation."

Sample Answer 2: "To encourage innovation, I advocate for dedicated time for team members to work on passion projects that align with our organizational goals. This approach has led to the development of several successful initiatives and solutions that originated from these projects, demonstrating the power of investing in creative freedom."

Fresh Graduate: Answer along the same lines as the sample answers above.

Q3: Describe an innovative project you initiated or were a part of. What was your role, and what was the outcome?

Explanation: This question aims to gather insights into your direct involvement with innovative projects and your ability to turn ideas into successful outcomes.

Sample Answer 1: "I initiated a project to automate our client reporting process, which was manual and time-consuming. As the project lead, I researched and implemented a software solution that not only automated the process but also provided deeper insights into our client data. The project improved efficiency by 50% and enhanced our decision-making capabilities."

Sample Answer 2: "As part of a team, I contributed to the development of a mobile app that addressed a common customer pain point. My role involved conducting user research and testing the app's usability to ensure it met customer needs. The app was well-received, leading to a significant increase in customer satisfaction and loyalty."

Fresh Graduate: Answer along the same lines as the sample answers above.

Q4: How do you approach risk-taking when it comes to implementing new ideas or innovations?

Explanation: This question explores your risk management strategy and your confidence in making bold decisions to drive innovation.

Sample Answer 1: "I approach risk-taking with a balance of caution and optimism. Before implementing new ideas, I conduct thorough research and feasibility studies to assess potential risks and rewards. I also consider small-scale pilots or prototypes to test ideas in a controlled environment, minimizing potential negative impacts while exploring innovative solutions."

Sample Answer 2: "Risk-taking is essential for innovation, but it must be informed. I evaluate the potential impact of new ideas against our team's and organization's strategic goals, considering both short-term challenges and long-term benefits. Clear communication and stakeholder buy-in are crucial steps in mitigating risks associated with implementing innovative solutions."

Fresh Graduate: Answer along the same lines as the sample answers above.

Q5: Can you give an example of a time when you had to pivot or change direction quickly in response to feedback or new information?

Explanation: Adaptability and the willingness to pivot are key traits in innovative thinking. Share a scenario where you demonstrated flexibility in your plans or ideas based on new insights.

Sample Answer 1: "During the beta testing of a new software feature, we received feedback indicating that users found it confusing and not as helpful as anticipated. I quickly gathered my team to reassess our approach, leading to a significant pivot in the feature's design. The revised feature, informed by user feedback, was much more successful and appreciated by our user base."

Sample Answer 2: "After launching a new marketing campaign, early metrics showed it was not performing as expected. I analyzed the data, sought feedback from the sales team, and realized our messaging was off target. We revised our campaign strategy accordingly, which resulted in a turnaround and exceeded our original performance goals."

Fresh Graduate: Answer along the same lines as the sample answers above.

Q6: How do you keep your team motivated during a long-term project with many challenges?

Explanation: This question explores your ability to maintain team morale and motivation, especially important in fostering a creative and innovative environment through challenging periods.

Sample Answer 1: "I keep the team motivated by setting short-term milestones and celebrating those achievements along the way. This creates a sense of progress and accomplishment. Additionally, I ensure open communication about the challenges we face and involve the team in problem-solving, which fosters a sense of ownership and commitment to the project's success."

Sample Answer 2: "I maintain motivation by focusing on the project's vision and the impact our work will have. Sharing positive feedback from stakeholders or customers can also boost morale. Moreover, recognizing individual contributions and providing opportunities for professional growth during the project keeps the team engaged and motivated."

Fresh Graduate: Answer along the same lines as the sample answers above.

Q7: What strategies do you use to encourage creative thinking within your team?

Explanation: This question assesses how you cultivate a creative atmosphere that encourages innovative thinking and problem-solving.

Sample Answer 1: "I encourage creative thinking by hosting regular brainstorming sessions where all ideas are welcomed and considered. To stimulate creativity, I sometimes introduce 'wild card' challenges unrelated to our current projects. This helps break routine thinking patterns and fosters a culture of innovation."

Sample Answer 2: "I've found that providing a safe space for experimentation is key to encouraging creativity. This means accepting that not all ideas will succeed but valuing the learning process. I also promote cross-functional collaboration, which brings diverse perspectives and enhances our creative problem-solving capabilities."

Fresh Graduate: Answer along the same lines as the sample answers above.

Q8: Describe a time when an unconventional approach led to a successful solution.

Explanation: Highlighting your willingness to explore unconventional paths can demonstrate your creative problem-solving skills and innovative thinking.

Sample Answer 1: "Facing a decline in customer engagement, I suggested an unconventional approach by launching a community-based marketing campaign, focusing on building relationships rather than direct sales. This strategy significantly increased engagement and customer loyalty, proving that thinking outside the traditional marketing tactics could yield great results."

Sample Answer 2: "When traditional methods failed to resolve a persistent software bug, I led the team in adopting a hackathon-style approach, dedicating a day to brainstorm and test out-of-the-box solutions. This not only solved the bug but also fostered a sense of teamwork and creativity within the team."

Fresh Graduate: Answer along the same lines as the sample answers above.

Q9: How do you balance the pursuit of new ideas with the constraints of budget and resources?

Explanation: This question explores your ability to manage innovation within the practical limitations of the workplace.

Sample Answer 1: "Balancing innovation with budget constraints involves careful prioritization and validation of ideas. I start with a thorough assessment to identify the most promising ideas with the potential for high impact. Implementing small-scale prototypes or pilots helps validate these ideas before committing significant resources."

Sample Answer 2: "I encourage the team to be resourceful and look for cost-effective ways to explore new ideas, such as leveraging existing tools in new ways or collaborating with external partners. Regular reviews ensure that our innovation efforts align with strategic goals and available resources, maximizing our ROI on new initiatives."

Fresh Graduate: Question not applicable.

Q10: How do you anticipate future trends in your industry, and how have you prepared your team to adapt to these changes?

Explanation: Employers are looking for forward-thinking candidates who can guide their teams through future industry shifts and challenges.

Sample Answer 1: "Anticipating future trends involves staying well-informed through industry research, attending conferences, and networking with thought leaders. I've prepared my team by fostering a culture of continuous learning and encouraging them to engage in professional development opportunities that align with these anticipated trends."

Sample Answer 2: "I use a combination of data analysis, customer feedback, and competitive intelligence to anticipate future trends. To prepare my team, we regularly discuss these trends and their potential impact during team meetings, and I allocate time and resources for skill development in areas that will be crucial for future success."

Fresh Graduate: "Anticipating future trends would require staying well-informed through industry research, attending conferences, and networking with thought leaders. I would encourage my team to foster a culture of continuous learning and to engage in professional development opportunities that align with these anticipated trends."

Chapter 9: Strategic Thinking and Vision

The ability to think strategically and have a clear vision for the future is invaluable in today's fast-paced business environment. In this chapter, we focus on your capacity to not only set long-term goals but also to devise and implement plans that align with the broader objectives of the organization. This chapter is designed to help you articulate your approach to strategic planning, decision-making, and how you envision and contribute to the future success of your team and the company at large.

Strategic thinkers are sought after for their ability to see the bigger picture, anticipate future challenges, and navigate through complexity with foresight and insight. This chapter will guide you on how to demonstrate your strategic approach and visionary thinking. making you an asset to any team, preparing you to effectively communicate your value to potential employers.

Q1: How do you align your team's goals with the company's strategic objectives?

Explanation: This question assesses your ability to ensure that your team's efforts contribute to the overall success of the organization. It's an opportunity to discuss your understanding of the company's vision and how you translate that into actionable plans for your team.

Sample Answer 1: "I align my team's goals with the company's strategic objectives by first ensuring a deep understanding of the company's vision and key priorities. I then set clear, measurable goals for my team that directly support those priorities, engaging in regular discussions to ensure our projects and initiatives are contributing to the broader organizational goals."

Sample Answer 2: "To ensure alignment, I maintain close communication with other departments and leadership to stay updated on the company's strategic direction. This allows me to adjust our team's focus and projects accordingly, ensuring that our work is always contributing to the company's overarching objectives. Regular team meetings focused on how our goals fit within the company's strategy reinforce this alignment."

Fresh Graduate: "Aligning goals with the company's strategic objectives requires complete comprehension of the company's vision and key priorities. I like to engage in regular discussions to ensure that our work is contributing to the broader organizational goals. "

Q2: Describe a strategic plan you developed and implemented. What was the outcome?

Explanation: Employers are looking for candidates who can not only strategize but also execute those strategies effectively. Share a specific example of your strategic planning process and its impact.

Sample Answer 1: "I developed a strategic plan to enter a new market segment that involved comprehensive market analysis, stakeholder engagement, and phased implementation. By focusing on key milestones and adapting our approach based on feedback and performance metrics, the plan was successful, resulting in a 20% increase in market share within the first year."

Sample Answer 2: "In response to emerging industry trends, I led the creation of a strategic plan to digitalize our customer service operations. This included implementing new technologies and training staff. The outcome was a significant improvement in customer satisfaction scores and operational efficiency, demonstrating the value of forward-thinking and strategic adaptation."

Fresh Graduate: Answer along the same lines as the sample answers above.

Q3: How do you ensure your decisions are data-driven?

Explanation: This question gauges your commitment to evidence-based decision-making, a critical component of strategic thinking. Highlight how you utilize data to inform your choices.

Sample Answer 1: "I ensure my decisions are data-driven by incorporating analytics into all stages of the decision-making process. This includes defining key performance indicators, collecting and analyzing relevant data, and using insights gained to guide my choices. Regularly reviewing outcomes against our predictions also helps refine future decisions."

Sample Answer 2: "For me, being data-driven means not just looking at the numbers but understanding the story they tell. I use a variety of data sources to inform my decisions, from market research to customer feedback and internal performance metrics. This comprehensive approach ensures that my decisions are well-rounded and supported by evidence."

Fresh Graduate: Answer along the same lines as the sample answers above.

Q4: How do you manage risk in strategic planning?

Explanation: Strategic planning often involves navigating uncertainty. This question explores how you identify, assess, and mitigate risks in your plans.

Sample Answer 1: "I manage risk in strategic planning by first conducting a thorough risk assessment for each component of the plan. This involves identifying potential risks, evaluating their likelihood and impact, and developing mitigation strategies. Regularly revisiting and updating the risk management plan is crucial as the project progresses and new information comes to light."

Sample Answer 2: "In managing risk, I emphasize the importance of flexibility in strategic plans. While we set clear goals and milestones, I also plan for contingencies, allowing us to adapt our approach in response to unexpected challenges. This flexibility, combined with ongoing risk monitoring, helps us navigate uncertainties more effectively."

Fresh Graduate: Answer along the same lines as the sample answers above.

Q5: Can you describe a time when you had to make a difficult strategic decision without all the information you needed?

Explanation: Decision-making under uncertainty tests your judgment and ability to act confidently with incomplete data. Share how you approached such a situation.

Sample Answer 1: "Faced with a tight deadline to decide on a significant investment, and without complete market analysis, I relied on available data, consulted with experts within the team, and drew on similar past decisions. I made the decision to proceed, which ultimately opened up a new revenue stream for the company, validating the importance of decisive action even with limited information."

Sample Answer 2: "When a competitor launched a disruptive new product, I had to quickly decide on our response with limited insight into their strategy. I gathered as much intelligence as possible, assessed our options based on our strengths, and decided to fast-track our R&D efforts to innovate beyond our competitor's offering. This decision required taking a calculated risk, but it paid off by solidifying our market leadership."

Fresh Graduate: "During my final year university project [or internship at a tech startup], I faced a situation where we had to choose a key feature for our app [or product] launch with incomplete user data. I quickly gathered insights from available sources, consulted with my team, and analyzed similar past projects. I proposed focusing on a feature that addressed a common user pain point. This decision resulted in positive feedback from our professors [or successful market reception], highlighting the importance of decisive action under uncertainty."

Q6: How do you prioritize projects and initiatives under your strategic plan?

Explanation: This question evaluates your ability to make decisions that align with strategic objectives, ensuring resources are allocated effectively.

Sample Answer 1: "I prioritize projects based on their alignment with our strategic goals, potential impact, and resource requirements. This involves a careful analysis and ranking of each project according to these criteria, followed by discussions with stakeholders to ensure a consensus on priorities. This method ensures our efforts are focused on what delivers the most value to the organization."

Sample Answer 2: "I use a scoring system to evaluate each project's relevance to our strategic objectives, its ROI, and urgency. Projects that score highest are prioritized for immediate action, while others may be scheduled for a later date or reassessed. Regularly revisiting these priorities ensures we adapt to changing circumstances and remain aligned with our strategic goals."

Fresh Graduate: Question not applicable.

Q7: Describe a situation where you had to adjust your strategy based on new information or results.

Explanation: Agility in strategic planning is crucial. Share an instance where you demonstrated flexibility in your strategic approach.

Sample Answer 1: "After launching a new product line, initial sales were below expectations despite positive market research. I led a review of our strategy and realized we had misjudged our target market's preferences. We quickly adjusted our marketing strategy to focus on a different demographic, which significantly improved our sales."

Sample Answer 2: "During an expansion strategy into a new market, early feedback indicated that our usual business model wasn't as effective in this region. Based on this new information, we pivoted our approach to a partnership model, collaborating with local businesses. This adjustment not only enhanced our market entry but also accelerated our growth in the region."

Fresh Graduate: During my group project in my final year of university, we were tasked with developing a business plan for a startup. Initially, we based our strategy on targeting college students as our primary market. However, halfway through the project, new survey data revealed that working professionals showed a higher interest in our product. We quickly adjusted our strategy to focus on this new demographic, revising our marketing plan and product features. This pivot led to more robust and compelling results, earning high praise from our professors. This experience taught me the importance of staying flexible and adapting strategies based on new information.

Q8: How do you communicate strategic plans and ensure buy-in from your team and stakeholders?

Explanation: Effective communication is key to successful strategic implementation. Illustrate how you ensure clarity, alignment, and commitment among all parties involved.

Sample Answer 1: "I communicate strategic plans by presenting a clear, compelling vision of what we aim to achieve and how each role contributes to these objectives. I involve key team members and stakeholders early in the planning process to gather input and build consensus, ensuring that the strategy is understood and embraced by all."

Sample Answer 2: "To ensure buy-in, I use a combination of formal presentations, detailed documentation, and regular updates to communicate our strategic plans. I emphasize the benefits and expected outcomes, addressing concerns and answering questions to clarify any ambiguities. Celebrating milestones and recognizing contributions also helps maintain enthusiasm and commitment."

Fresh Graduate: "During my final year university project [or internship at a tech company], I communicated our strategic plans by organizing an initial team meeting to outline our goals and the importance of each member's role. I used visual aids and clear examples to illustrate our vision, encouraging open discussion for feedback and concerns. Regular updates and progress reports kept everyone informed, while celebrating small wins helped maintain motivation and commitment. This approach ensured clarity, alignment, and enthusiastic buy-in from the team and stakeholders."

Q9: How do you measure the success of your strategic initiatives?

Explanation: This question explores your approach to evaluating performance and determining the effectiveness of strategic actions.

Sample Answer 1: "I measure the success of strategic initiatives through key performance indicators (KPIs) that are established at the outset. These KPIs are directly linked to strategic goals and provide quantifiable measures of progress. Regular reviews against these metrics, along with qualitative feedback from customers and team members, inform us of our success and areas for improvement."

Sample Answer 2: "Success is measured by comparing our outcomes against the specific objectives we set at the beginning of the initiative. This includes both quantitative metrics, such as revenue growth or market share, and qualitative outcomes, like improved brand perception. I also consider the lessons learned and the process improvements made as key indicators of success, as they contribute to our long-term capabilities."

Fresh Graduate: "As a fresh graduate, I measure the success of strategic initiatives by setting clear, achievable goals at the start, like project milestones and deliverables. I track progress by regularly comparing our actual results with these goals. Additionally, I seek feedback from my team and supervisors to understand the impact of our work and identify areas for improvement. This approach helps me learn and adapt, ensuring that we stay on track and achieve our objectives effectively."

Q10: Can you discuss a time when you had to lead your team through a significant change or pivot in strategy? How did you manage the transition?

Explanation: This question assesses your leadership in guiding teams through uncertainty and change, crucial for maintaining momentum and focus.

Sample Answer 1: "When our company decided to pivot from a product-centric to a customer-centric strategy, it required a significant mindset shift for the team. I managed the transition by clearly communicating the reasons behind the change, involving the team in redefining our processes, and providing training to develop new skills. Regular check-ins and an open-door policy for addressing concerns helped ease the transition, ultimately leading to a more adaptive and customer-focused team culture."

Sample Answer 2: "Faced with emerging competition, we had to rapidly shift our market strategy to remain competitive. I led my team through this pivot by outlining the new strategic direction and what it meant for our projects. By fostering a collaborative environment where the team could contribute ideas on how to execute this new strategy, we maintained engagement and ownership, making the transition smoother and more effective."

Fresh Graduate: "During my final year university group project [or internship at a startup], we had to pivot our strategy midway through due to new research findings that changed our project's direction. As the team lead, I managed the transition by first explaining the reasons behind the change and how it would benefit our project. I encouraged open discussions to address any concerns and gather input on how to best implement the new strategy. By clearly defining new roles and responsibilities and setting up regular check-ins to monitor progress, I ensured that everyone stayed aligned and motivated. This approach helped us successfully adapt to the new direction and achieve our project goals."

Chapter 10: Personal Insights and Reflections

The journey through an interview process is not only about showcasing your professional achievements and competencies but also about providing a window into who you are as a person. This chapter is designed to help you articulate your values, motivations, and the unique perspectives you bring to the workplace. Here, we will delve into questions that may seem less technical but are equally crucial in painting a holistic picture of yourself as a well-rounded candidate.

Employers are increasingly valuing emotional intelligence, resilience, adaptability, and cultural fit. Through this chapter, you'll explore how to communicate your personal growth experiences, lessons learned through challenges, and your approach to work-life balance and continuous self-improvement. It's an opportunity to connect with potential employers on a more personal level and show how your unique blend of skills, experiences, and personality traits make you the ideal candidate for their team.

Q1: What motivates you to come to work every day?

Explanation: This question seeks to uncover your intrinsic motivations and passion for your work. Reflect on what drives you beyond the paycheck.

Sample Answer 1: "What motivates me to come to work every day is the opportunity to solve new challenges and make a tangible impact through my work. Knowing that I'm contributing to something larger than myself, especially in a collaborative environment where ideas and efforts are valued, is incredibly rewarding."

Sample Answer 2: "I'm motivated by the continuous learning opportunities my field offers. Every day is a chance to grow my skills and knowledge, which not only benefits my personal development but also allows me to contribute more effectively to my team and the company's goals."

Fresh Graduate: "I am motivated by the opportunity to tackle new challenges and contribute to meaningful projects. The chance to learn continuously, work collaboratively with my team, and see the impact of our work drives me. Knowing that I am part of a team working towards a larger goal makes every day rewarding."

Q2: How do you manage stress and maintain work-life balance?

Explanation: This question assesses your self-awareness and strategies for ensuring personal well-being while meeting professional responsibilities.

Sample Answer 1: "I manage stress by maintaining a healthy work-life balance through regular exercise, spending time with family and friends, and pursuing hobbies that I enjoy. Additionally, I prioritize and delegate tasks effectively at work, ensuring I don't become overwhelmed and can perform at my best."

Sample Answer 2: "I've found that setting clear boundaries between work and personal time is key to managing stress. I also practice mindfulness and meditation to stay centered and focused. Staying organized and proactive about managing my workload helps prevent stress from becoming overwhelming."

Fresh Graduate: "I maintain work-life balance by setting clear boundaries between work and personal time. I prioritize tasks and use tools like to-do lists to stay organized. I also make time for activities I enjoy, such as exercising, reading, and spending time with friends and family, which helps me stay refreshed and focused."

Q3: What is your approach to personal and professional development?

Explanation: Employers are interested in how you take initiative in your growth. Share your strategies for continuous learning and improvement.

Sample Answer 1: "My approach to personal and professional development is rooted in setting specific, achievable goals and actively seeking opportunities to expand my skills and knowledge. Whether it's through formal education, mentorship, or challenging projects, I'm always looking for ways to push my boundaries and grow."

Sample Answer 2: "I believe in the power of feedback for personal and professional development. I regularly seek constructive feedback from colleagues and supervisors, reflecting on it and turning it into actionable steps for improvement. Staying open to new experiences and learning from both successes and failures are also integral to my growth."

Fresh Graduate: "My approach to development is to set specific goals and seek out opportunities to expand my skills. I attend workshops, webinars, and take online courses to keep learning. I also value feedback from mentors and peers, using it to improve and take on new challenges that help me grow both personally and professionally."

Q4: Describe a failure you experienced and what you learned from it.

Explanation: This question explores your resilience and ability to learn from mistakes. A thoughtful reflection on a past failure can demonstrate maturity and growth.

Sample Answer 1: "One of my projects failed to meet its objectives due to a misalignment in team communication. This experience taught me the critical importance of clear, continuous communication and regular check-ins with all team members. It was a valuable lesson in teamwork and project management that has since informed my approach to leading projects."

Sample Answer 2: "Early in my career, I missed a crucial deadline that impacted our team's schedule. This failure highlighted the importance of time management and realistic goal-setting. I learned to better organize my workload, set more achievable deadlines, and communicate early if a deadline is at risk."

Fresh Graduate: Answer along the same lines as the sample answers above.

Q5: How do you approach making difficult decisions?

Explanation: Decision-making is a critical skill. This question assesses your process for making tough choices, especially when faced with limited information or competing interests.

Sample Answer 1: "When making difficult decisions, I first gather as much information as possible and weigh the potential outcomes. I also consult with relevant stakeholders to gain different perspectives. Ultimately, I rely on a combination of data-driven analysis and my intuition, grounded in my experiences, to make the best decision possible."

Sample Answer 2: "I approach difficult decisions with a structured methodology, evaluating the pros and cons of each option and considering the impact on all involved parties. Transparency and open communication during the decision-making process help build trust and understanding, even when the decision is tough."

Fresh Graduate: Answer along the same lines as the sample answers above.

Q6: What do you consider your most significant professional achievement, and why?

Explanation: This question allows you to share a milestone that holds personal significance, offering insights into your values and what you consider important in your work.

Sample Answer 1: "My most significant professional achievement was leading a project that not only exceeded our financial goals but also won an industry award for innovation. This accomplishment stands out to me because it was a testament to our team's hard work, creativity, and resilience, embodying my belief in the power of collaboration and innovation."

Sample Answer 2: "Launching a community outreach program within my organization that has since become a staple of our corporate social responsibility efforts is what I'm most proud of. It's significant to me because it aligns with my personal values of giving back and demonstrates how businesses can make a real difference in their communities."

Fresh Graduate: Answer along the same lines as the sample answers above.

Q7: How do you handle criticism or feedback?

Explanation: Your response to feedback is indicative of your openness to growth and ability to engage constructively with others, even in challenging situations.

Sample Answer 1: "I welcome criticism and feedback as essential elements of personal and professional development. I listen carefully, ask questions for clarity, and reflect on the feedback to identify actionable steps I can take to improve. This approach has helped me grow and strengthen my skills over time."

Sample Answer 2: "Handling criticism with an open mind has always been my approach. I view feedback as an opportunity to gain insights that I might have overlooked. By separating my emotions from the constructive aspects of the feedback, I can use it as a tool for continuous improvement."

Fresh Graduate: Answer along the same lines as the sample answers above.

Q8: Can you share an experience where you went above and beyond for a project or team?

Explanation: This question explores your dedication and willingness to put in extra effort when needed, revealing your commitment to achieving excellence.

Sample Answer 1: "On a critical project with a tight deadline, I noticed my team was struggling with burnout. I organized a series of workshops to streamline our processes and volunteered for extra tasks to alleviate their workload. My initiative not only helped us meet our deadline but also improved team morale and productivity for future projects."

Sample Answer 2: "When a key client threatened to take their business elsewhere due to dissatisfaction with a previous project, I took it upon myself to rebuild that relationship. I conducted in-depth research into their concerns, proposed a new project plan addressing those issues, and led the project to successful completion, ultimately retaining the client and securing future business."

Fresh Graduate: "During my final year university group project, we faced a major setback when a critical part of our research data was lost a week before the submission deadline. I took the initiative to stay late in the lab and worked through the weekend to redo the experiments and gather the necessary data. I also coordinated with my team to ensure everyone was on the same page and motivated. My extra effort and dedication helped us complete the project on time, and we received high praise for our work. This experience reinforced my commitment to going above and beyond to achieve success."

Q9: What aspects of your work are you most passionate about, and why?

Explanation: This question aims to uncover what drives your enthusiasm and commitment in your professional life, providing a glimpse into what motivates and fulfills you.

Sample Answer 1: "I'm most passionate about solving complex problems that have a direct impact on our customers' satisfaction. The challenge of untangling intricate issues and the tangible results of improving someone's experience with our product is incredibly rewarding and motivates me to continually strive for excellence."

Sample Answer 2: "I find great passion in mentoring and developing younger team members. Seeing their growth and knowing I played a part in their professional journey is deeply fulfilling. It's a reminder of the impact we can have on others beyond just meeting business objectives."

Fresh Graduate: "I'm most passionate about the opportunity to learn and grow through hands-on experiences. I love tackling new challenges and acquiring new skills that help me contribute to my team and projects. The excitement of applying my knowledge to real-world situations and seeing the tangible impact of my work keeps me motivated and engaged."

Q10: How do you envision your career evolving in the next five years?

Explanation: This question assesses your ambition, career planning, and how your future goals align with the position and company you're interviewing with.

Sample Answer 1: "In the next five years, I see myself advancing to a leadership role where I can have a greater impact on strategic decision-making and mentorship within the company. I plan to deepen my expertise in my field and develop my leadership skills to contribute to the company's growth and success on a larger scale."

Sample Answer 2: "I envision my career evolving towards a specialization in emerging technologies within our industry. I aim to be at the forefront of implementing innovative solutions that can drive our company forward. Over the next five years, I plan to engage in continuous learning and take on challenging projects to prepare myself for this role."

Fresh Graduate: "In the next five years, I envision myself growing into a more specialized role within my field, where I can leverage the skills and knowledge I've gained to make a significant impact. I plan to pursue further certifications and training to deepen my expertise, and I hope to take on more responsibilities in projects that drive innovation and efficiency. Ultimately, I aim to contribute to the company's success and be part of a dynamic team that values continuous learning and growth."

Bonus Chapter: Top 10 Questions for Freshers

Transitioning from the academic world to the professional arena is a significant milestone. This bonus chapter is tailored for freshers stepping out of college or university and embarking on their journey into the workforce. It focuses on the most common questions fresh graduates face during interviews, providing insights into how to present your academic experiences, projects, internships, and extracurricular activities in a way that showcases your potential as a promising candidate.

Employers looking to hire freshers are interested in your learning ability, adaptability, enthusiasm, and how you can contribute with fresh perspectives. Through this chapter, you'll learn to articulate your strengths, aspirations, and readiness to tackle the professional challenges ahead, even with limited work experience.

Q1: How have your academic experiences prepared you for this role?

Explanation: Highlight the relevant courses, projects, or research you've undertaken that provide a foundation for the role you're applying for.

Sample Answer 1: "My academic experiences, particularly in software development projects and internships, have equipped me with a strong foundation in coding, problem-solving, and teamwork. These skills are directly applicable to the role, where I can further develop them in a professional setting."

Sample Answer 2: "During my degree, I engaged in extensive research on consumer behavior, which involved analyzing data and trends. This has prepared me to contribute to the marketing team with insights on target market strategies and improving customer engagement."

Q2: What extracurricular activities were you involved in, and what skills did you gain from them?

Explanation: This question explores your interests outside academics and how they have contributed to your personal and professional development.

Sample Answer 1: "I was an active member of the debate club, which honed my public speaking and critical thinking skills. These experiences taught me the value of clear communication and persuasive argumentation, skills that are beneficial in any professional context."

Sample Answer 2: "As captain of the university soccer team, I developed leadership and team coordination skills. Managing team dynamics, strategizing game plans, and motivating team members are competencies that I can bring to a collaborative workplace."

Q3: Describe a challenging project or assignment you worked on. What was your role, and what was the outcome?

Explanation: Discuss a specific academic or extracurricular project that showcases your problem-solving abilities and work ethic.

Sample Answer 1: "For my final year project, I led a team to develop a mobile app that addressed a local community issue. My role involved project management, from ideation through to development and testing. The successful launch of the app demonstrated our ability to turn concepts into practical solutions."

Sample Answer 2: "I undertook an assignment to analyze the impact of digital marketing strategies on small businesses. I conducted interviews, compiled data, and presented findings that offered actionable insights. This project sharpened my analytical skills and my ability to communicate complex information clearly."

Q4: How do you plan to compensate for your lack of professional experience?

Explanation: Acknowledge the gap while emphasizing your eagerness to learn, adaptability, and transferable skills from your academic and extracurricular experiences.

Sample Answer 1: "I plan to leverage my strong academic foundation and eagerness to learn quickly on the job. My internships and project work have equipped me with a basic understanding of the industry, and I'm committed to taking on challenges that will accelerate my professional growth."

Sample Answer 2: "I intend to compensate for my lack of professional experience with my proactive attitude and ability to adapt. I have demonstrated these qualities through various leadership roles in university clubs and volunteer work, showing my capability to contribute positively and learn rapidly in new environments."

Q5: What do you consider your biggest achievement during your college/university years?

Explanation: Share an achievement that reflects your dedication, skills, or leadership potential.

Sample Answer 1: "My biggest achievement was organizing a campus-wide tech hackathon, which saw participation from over 200 students. Managing this event from planning to execution taught me valuable project management and organizational skills, and the success of the event was a testament to our team's hard work."

Sample Answer 2: "Graduating at the top of my class while balancing extracurricular commitments was my biggest achievement. It demonstrated my ability to manage time effectively, prioritize tasks, and maintain a high standard of work across different areas of my life."

Q6: How do you handle receiving constructive criticism?

Explanation: This question evaluates your openness to feedback and ability to use it for personal and professional growth.

Sample Answer 1: "I welcome constructive criticism as it provides me with an opportunity to improve. I listen carefully, ask questions for clarity, and reflect on the feedback to identify actionable steps. This approach has helped me enhance my skills and become more effective in my role."

Sample Answer 2: "Receiving constructive criticism is crucial for my development. I approach it with an open mind and gratitude for the chance to improve. After receiving feedback, I often seek advice on how to address the areas of concern and make a concerted effort to apply what I've learned."

Q7: Can you describe a time when you went above and beyond for your job or a project?

Explanation: Employers appreciate employees who show dedication and willingness to exceed expectations.

Sample Answer 1: "On a key project with a tight deadline, I realized we were at risk of falling short. I coordinated a series of extra work sessions for the team and liaised with other departments to ensure we had the resources needed. My extra effort ensured the project was not only completed on time but also exceeded our client's expectations."

Sample Answer 2: " During my final year group project at university, we were tasked with developing a complex presentation for a competition. Realizing we were behind schedule and the quality wasn't meeting our standards, I organized extra meetings and worked long hours to enhance our research and presentation. I also took the lead in contacting industry experts for insights and feedback. My extra effort not only helped us meet the deadline but also led to us winning the competition, which was a major achievement for our team."

Q8: What are your long-term career goals?

Explanation: This question explores your future aspirations and how the position aligns with your career trajectory.

Sample Answer 1: "My long-term goal is to progress to a leadership position where I can contribute to strategic decision-making and mentor the next generation of professionals in my field. I see this role as a crucial step in that journey, offering the opportunity to develop the necessary skills and experiences."

Sample Answer 2: "I aim to become an expert in my field, known for my ability to tackle complex challenges and drive innovation. I'm particularly interested in roles that allow me to continuously learn and take on increasing responsibilities. This position aligns perfectly with those goals, providing a solid foundation for growth."

Q9: How do you balance teamwork with independence in your work?

Explanation: This question assesses your ability to work autonomously while being an effective team player.

Sample Answer 1: "I balance teamwork and independence by clearly understanding my role within the team and the objectives we're collectively aiming to achieve. I take initiative on tasks I can complete independently but always keep the lines of communication open for collaboration and feedback."

Sample Answer 2: "While I value independence and the ability to complete tasks on my own, I also recognize the importance of collaboration and diverse perspectives. I strive to contribute my strengths to team efforts while being open to learning from my colleagues, finding this balance leads to more robust and successful outcomes."

Q10: How do you stay motivated in your work?

Explanation: Understanding what drives you provides insight into your values and how they align with the company's culture.

Sample Answer 1: "I stay motivated by setting personal and professional goals and reflecting on my progress towards these. Engaging in challenging projects that push my boundaries and allow me to grow also keeps me motivated, as does seeing the tangible impact of my work on the company and its clients."

Sample Answer 2: "My motivation comes from a passion for my field and the satisfaction of solving problems and making a difference. Continuous learning and the opportunity to apply new knowledge and skills to real-world challenges keep me engaged and excited about my work."

Actionable Tips and Strategies for Interview Preparation

Researching the Company:

- Visit the company's website, focusing on the "About Us," "News," and "Careers" sections to understand their values, mission, and recent achievements.

- Use LinkedIn to research the company's culture, key employees, and recent posts or announcements.

- Look for recent articles about the company in industry publications to gain insights into their market position and future directions.

Dressing for Success:

- Understand the company's dress code by researching their social media or asking the HR representative, and dress one level up from their daily wear.

- Opt for classic and neutral colors to ensure a professional appearance.

- Ensure your clothes are clean, well-fitted, and ironed. Personal grooming is equally important.

Following Up After an Interview:

- Send a personalized thank you email to each interviewer within 24 hours, expressing appreciation for their time and reiterating your interest in the role.

- If feedback or a decision timeline was not discussed during the interview, it's appropriate to include a polite inquiry in your follow-up.
- Use this opportunity to briefly mention any relevant skills or experiences you didn't get a chance to discuss during the interview.

Managing Interview Nerves:

- Prepare thoroughly: The more you know about the company and the more you practice your answers, the more confident you will feel.
- Practice mindfulness or deep-breathing exercises to calm your nerves before the interview.
- Remember that it's okay to take a moment to think before answering a question. You can also ask to return to a question later if you need time to gather your thoughts.
- Visualize success before the interview to boost your confidence and reduce anxiety.

Additional Tips:

- Always have questions prepared to ask the interviewer. This shows your interest in the role and the company.
- Practice your body language. Maintain good posture, eye contact, and a friendly, confident demeanor throughout the interview.

- Familiarize yourself with common interview formats (behavioral, case studies, technical tests) relevant to your field and prepare accordingly.

- Keep a portfolio of your work or achievements handy, if relevant, to provide tangible examples of your skills and accomplishments.

Incorporating these tips and strategies into your interview preparation can significantly improve your performance and increase your chances of making a positive impression. Remember, preparation and practice are key to interview success.

Personal Development Plan Template

Personal Information

- Name:
- Date:
- Career Goal(s):

Self-Assessment

- **Strengths:** List your key professional strengths and how they align with your career goals.
- **Areas for Improvement:** Identify skills or areas you need to improve to achieve your career goals or enhance your interview performance.
- **Opportunities:** Note any upcoming opportunities for professional development, such as projects, courses, or networking events.
- **Challenges:** Acknowledge any obstacles that might hinder your progress and think of ways to overcome them.

Skills and Competencies

- **Technical Skills:** List the technical skills required for your desired role and rate your proficiency in each.
- **Soft Skills:** Identify essential soft skills (e.g., communication, teamwork, leadership) needed for success in your field and self-assess your competence.

- **Interview Skills:** Reflect on your current interview skills, including areas such as articulating your strengths, addressing weaknesses, and asking insightful questions.

Goals and Actions

1. **Short-term Goals (Next 3-6 Months)**
   - Goal 1:
     - Action Steps:
     - Resources Needed:
     - Deadline:
   - Goal 2:
     - Action Steps:
     - Resources Needed:
     - Deadline:

2. **Long-term Goals (1-3 Years)**
   - Goal 1:
     - Action Steps:
     - Resources Needed:
     - Deadline:
   - Goal 2:
     - Action Steps:
     - Resources Needed:
     - Deadline:

Professional Development Activities

- **Courses/Training:** Identify relevant courses or training programs that will help improve your skills.
- **Reading:** List books, articles, or other materials related to your field or personal growth.
- **Networking:** Plan networking activities, such as attending industry events or joining professional groups.
- **Mentorship:** Consider finding a mentor or coach who can guide you in your professional development.

Feedback and Reflection

- **Feedback Sources:** Note individuals (e.g., mentors, peers, supervisors) who can provide constructive feedback on your progress.
- **Reflection:** Schedule regular intervals (e.g., monthly, quarterly) to reflect on your progress, reassess your goals, and adjust your plan as necessary.

Signature and Date

I commit to working on the above goals and actions to enhance my interview skills and achieve my professional growth objectives.

- **Signature:**
- **Date:**

Conclusion

As you reach the end of "Interview Genius: Master the 100 Toughest Questions & Land Your Dream Job," it's time to reflect on the wealth of knowledge you've gained and how it can transform your interview experiences. This guide has been crafted to give you the confidence and skills to tackle even the most challenging interview questions, but remember, every interview is a unique scenario.

Key Takeaways:

1. **Preparation is Key**: Thorough preparation builds confidence. Know your resume, research the company, and practice your answers.

2. **Authenticity Matters**: Be genuine in your responses. Employers value honesty and authenticity.

3. **Continuous Improvement**: Learn from each interview. Reflect on what went well and identify areas for improvement.

4. **Stay Positive**: A positive attitude can make a significant difference. Stay motivated and resilient, even in the face of setbacks.

While this book provides a solid foundation, it's essential to tailor your responses to each unique situation you encounter. The strategies and examples provided here are starting points—adapt them to fit your experiences, strengths, and the specific context of the job you're applying for. Your authenticity and personal touch are what will truly set you apart.

Personalize Your Approach:

- **Analyze the Job Description**: Understand the key competencies and tailor your answers to highlight your relevant skills and experiences.

- **Research the Company**: Align your responses with the company's values, mission, and current projects to demonstrate your enthusiasm and fit.

- **Reflect on Your Experiences**: Use real-life examples that showcase your unique journey and professional growth.

Final Words of Encouragement:

As you step into each interview, remember that it's not just about answering questions; it's about engaging in a meaningful conversation about your future. Approach each opportunity with enthusiasm and confidence, knowing that you have the tools to succeed. Your career journey is unique, and every interview is a steppingstone towards achieving your goals.

Thank you for letting "Interview Genius" be a part of your preparation. We wish you immense success in your interviews and the exciting opportunities that lie ahead. Here's to mastering your interviews and landing your dream job!

www.ingramcontent.com/pod-product-compliance
Lightning Source LLC
Chambersburg PA
CBHW071931210526
45479CB00002B/638